Praise for *It's Not What You Think*

"Jeff has written another terrific book that rattled more of my assumptions about Jesus. This is a good book, by a trusted friend about an awesome God who doesn't play by the rules we keep trying to give Him."

— Bob Goff, *New York Times* bestselling author of *Love Does*

"In this new book, Jefferson Bethke gives us a brisk, readable overview of the story of God's reconciling project with the universe. You will benefit from thinking with him about such grand topics in an enjoyable conversational format."

— Russell Moore, president, Southern Baptist Ethics and Religious Liberty Commission

"With a deep discernment of the times we're living in, Jefferson spotlights many misinterpreted truths in the Bible and puts a voice to the true heart of God's Word. His desire to bring us into a more intimate encounter with God jumps off of each page. Christians need this book—now more than ever!"

— Lysa TerKeurst, *New York Times* bestselling author of *The Best Yes* and president of Proverbs 31 Ministries

D0059069

"It's easy to get stuck in life. To let our faith grow stagnant, our walk grow weary, and our hope grow silent. Jefferson isn't okay with that and has created a book that turns what we think we know upside down. Creative, honest, refreshing. I'm a huge fan of the heart that explodes from this book."

— Jon Acuff, *New York Times* bestselling author of *Do Over: Rescue Monday, Reinvent Your Work & Never Get Stuck*

"This book is a challenge to me in my walk. It has pushed me to dig deeper then the surface level. I have realized that you can't just take bits and pieces of the Bible, but you have to take the whole thing in order to continue to grow. The lessons that we grow up learning in church are lessons we need to continue to focus on and grow in. Thank you, Jefferson, for opening my eyes to think deeper, and grow stronger."

— Sadie Robertson, *New York Times* bestselling author of *Live Original* and member of hit show *Duck Dynasty*

"My generation knows the basics of Christianity, but Jefferson sheds new light on these important truths. He challenges us to dig deeper, reminds us 'it's not (always) what you think.'"

— Chip Gaines, host of HGTV's hit show *Fixer Upper*

"Jefferson Bethke has done it again. His passion for sharing the power of Jesus shines through in *It's Not What You Think*. For so long Christians have been looking at the life of Jesus as an expensive vase they're scared to touch. Bethke shatters that perspective and re-introduces us to the Jesus who truly turned the world upside-down."

— Christine Caine, founder of the A21 Campaign and Propel Women

"Another thought provoking book by Jefferson. He brought up a lot of questions that still kept me wondering. I wasn't satisfied, in a good way. It made me want to dig deeper, not to just discover answers, but discover my relationship with Jesus."

— Candace Cameron Bure,
actress, producer, and *New York Times* bestselling author of *Reshaping It All*

"The striking thing about Jesus was that he entered a religious world and presented a simple, relational message of how to connect with God and what it meant to follow Him. Jefferson reminds me of Jesus in this way. He brings us back to what is simple and pure and lovely and strips away the excess that we have often created in our modern religious system. Prepare to enjoy God again and know Him in different ways."

— Jennie Allen, author of
Anything, founder and
visionary of IF:Gathering

"What a rare gift Jefferson has: to soak the believer in a new way of thinking while simultaneously welcoming those who know nothing of his faith. I've been impacted so deeply by his words, his convictions, his heart for the Lord, and his passion for the bride of Christ. Open the pages and find Jesus—the true Jesus—here."

— Angie Smith, author of
Seamless

IT'S NOT
WHAT YOU
THINK

IT'S NOT
WHAT YOU
THINK

WHY CHRISTIANITY IS ABOUT SO MUCH MORE THAN GOING TO HEAVEN WHEN YOU DIE

Jefferson Bethke

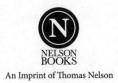

NELSON
BOOKS

An Imprint of Thomas Nelson

© 2015 by Jefferson Bethke

All rights reserved. No portion of this book may be reproduced, stored in a retrieval system, or transmitted in any form or by any means—electronic, mechanical, photocopy, recording, scanning, or other—except for brief quotations in critical reviews or articles, without the prior written permission of the publisher.

Published in Nashville, Tennessee, by Nelson Books, an imprint of Thomas Nelson. Nelson Books and Thomas Nelson are registered trademarks of HarperCollins Christian Publishing, Inc.

Published in association with Yates & Yates, www.yates2.com.

Thomas Nelson titles may be purchased in bulk for educational, business, fund-raising, or sales promotional use. For information, please e-mail SpecialMarkets@ThomasNelson.com.

Unless otherwise noted, Scripture quotations are taken from THE ENGLISH STANDARD VERSION. © 2001 by Crossway Bibles, a division of Good News Publishers.

Scripture marked NIV is taken from the Holy Bible, New International Version®, NIV®. Copyright © 1973, 1978, 1984, 2011 by Biblica, Inc.™ Used by permission of Zondervan. All rights reserved worldwide. www.zondervan.com

ISBN 978-0-7180-7984-0 (SE)

Library of Congress Cataloging-in-Publication Data

Bethke, Jefferson.
  It's not what you think: why Christianity is about so much more than going to heaven when you die / Jefferson Bethke.
    pages cm
  Includes bibliographical references.
  ISBN 978-1-4002-0541-7
  1. Christianity—Essence, genius, nature. 2. Theology, Doctrinal—Popular works.
  3. Christian life. I. Title.
  BT60.B4795 2015
    230—dc23   2015010663

Printed in the United States of America

15 16 17 18 19 RRD 6 5 4 3 2 1

For Kinsley:
I pray you come to know this beautiful
and life-giving Jesus as the pursuit of your entire life.
Daddy and Mommy love you so much.

CONTENTS

CONTENTS

FOREWORD

STRAIGHT UP—THE GUY JUST LIKED THE FRAME.

Four bucks.

That's all this guy had to dig out of wallet at that flea market in Adamstown, Pennsylvania, that morning in 1989 to buy one old, odd picture frame.

He handed over the four dollars and frankly didn't care one wit about the painting, a dismal little country scene dabbed across a grimy, torn canvas with a signature he couldn't even make out. It was the gilded and ornate frame that caught his eye.

The flea market seller took his four bucks—with absolutely no idea. With not the faintest idea that the frame and painting—*were not at all what you'd think.*

When the guy got home? The crudely made frame pathetically fell apart in his hands. Unsalvageable.

Great—four bucks wasted on a bunch of garbage.

But when the unsalvageable frame fell apart in his hands, fell away from the torn canvas?

There—between the slashed canvas and the wood backing of the crumbled frame—was this crisp, folded-up piece of paper, the size of a business envelope.

He unfolded it slowly. Ran his finger across the inked calligraphy.

It couldn't be what it read—*or was it?*

When a friend who collected historical memorabilia dropped by, he took out that crisp piece of paper, unfolded it slowly, for him to take a look at it. Laughed a bit when his friend shook his head, mouth agape.

"Well—what do you think?"

"Get it appraised."

Turns out?

That folded up piece of paper, one-tenth of an inch thick, that had fallen out between a torn canvas and a falling-apart frame was printed by John Dunlap. *On July 4, 1776.*

Turns out that it's one of only five hundred copies of the first printing of—*the Declaration of Independence.*

Turns out only twenty-three copies are known to still exist, of which only a mere two were privately owned—and then this one. *A flea market find.*

That copy was auctioned off on June 4, 1991—and when the gavel finally sounded "Sold!"—that four buck flea market frame had become a 2.4 million dollar find.

And that's not the only time it's happened.

Stan Caffy, a pipe fitter, bought a copy of the Declaration of Independence at a yard sale in Donelson Hills in 1996. He nailed it to the wall of his garage. He thought it was a dime-a-dozen dollar-store copy. *Not everything is what you think it is.*

The piece of faded paper hung there on the garage wall for ten years, while Stan fixed a steady stream of old bicycles.

Till finally Stan's wife, Linda, said it was time for Stan to clean out the garage. "I used to be a packrat," Stan admitted. "The best I can recall, we had a little debate about whether to keep it—that copy up on the wall or donate it—and Linda won."

So Linda took an antique table, a shower-massage-head, and a faucet—and the supposed everyday copy of the Declaration of Independence—to the Music City Thrift Store in Nashville on a morning in March.

Where Michael Sparks ended up browsing and stumbled upon this yellowed, shellacked, rolled-up piece of paper.

Two bucks and forty-eight cents. That's all Michael Sparks had to shell out for the document.

Which turned out to be?

One of the two hundred official copies of the Declaration of Independence that had been commissioned by John Quincy Adams in 1820.

Which turned out to be sold at an auction for—$477,650. *Nearly half a million dollars.*

When Stan heard? All he could say was:

"I'm happy for that Michael Sparks guy.

"If I still had it, it would still be hanging here in the garage and I still wouldn't know it was worth all that . . .

"But . . . can't help but feel not very smart."

Turns out?

You can have in your possession an actual declaration of freedom—*and not actually value it.*

You can hold in your hands something valuable enough that it could change everything about your life—*and you could send it right out of your life.*

You can think *you know* what to think—and it turns out: *it's not what you think.*

Maybe that's the whole point?

You don't think Jesus is your everything—*until you have nothing but Jesus.*

You don't think of Jesus as anything but ultimately *useful* to getting the life you want—until you experience Jesus as ultimately *the most beautiful* in the life you *already have.*

When you become God's, all duty becomes beauty.

You don't think of Jesus as anything but an example to follow—*until you experience Him as a Lover to fall into, as a Lamb to forgive you, as your Lord to free you.*

Like having an exorbitantly valuable declaration of freedom in your hands but not thinking you do, Christianity is not what you think:

Christianity is more than going to heaven when you die; it's about *dying* with Christ *now—so you can live now.*

Christianity is more than performing a good life—it's about Christ performing an *entirely perfect life for you*—so you can live the *abundant life in its entirety.*

Christianity is more than going through the motions—it's about letting Christ touch *the heart of your emotions*—*and going through life with Him.*

And in these pages that's what happens:

Jefferson Bethke authenticates the real deal of Christianity.

He tears back the worn canvas of religiosity, lets an unsalvageable, cheap frame of distractions fall away—and he unfolds for us the breathtaking *meaningfulness* and *worth* and *value* of authentically living with Christ.

He hands you these pages. This is your own declaration of freedom.

He makes you not miss the life-changing value of your declaration of freedom.

Because who can afford to live a life of missing Him?

We're tired of missing Him. Dismissing Him. Belittling Him—and living little.

It's time to check behind the cheap frame of things—because it turns out:

It's not what you think.

It's infinitely more.

Ann Voskamp,
June 2015
Author of the *New York Times*
bestsellers: *One Thousand Gifts:*
A Dare to Live Fully Right Where
You Are, The Greatest Gift, and
Unwrapping the Greatest Gift

INTRODUCTION

LIVING IN COLOR

IF YOU WENT TO A PUBLIC MIDDLE SCHOOL, YOU PROBABLY read a few classics for English class. I remember reading *To Kill a Mockingbird* and *Of Mice and Men*, among others. Hands down, though, my favorite novel was Lois Lowry's *The Giver* (which was recently made into a movie).

If you're not familiar with it, the basic premise is that an entire society is controlled by a group of elders who set up a system that strips all choices and emotions from humans' lives. Each human is forced to take an injection every morning that takes away these things.

Both the book and the movie communicate this by everyone living and seeing only black and white as the normal standard. There's no color, no life, no joy. But because of the injections, and because *everyone* takes them, they don't know that's not normal. They believe the world is black and white, and that it's devoid of colors and the blessings that come with them, and it's simply the way to live.

The main character, Jonas, starts to dream and have faint visions in color. He couldn't even describe what he thought he saw, but when he stops taking his injections fully, *everything* begins to show up in color. It's so radically life-giving and beautiful, he doesn't have language for what he's seeing. It's too vibrant and hypnotizing. Nothing changed about the world he is living in, except now his eyes have become able to perceive what was always there. He quickly and clearly realizes the world wasn't what he thought.

I believe the Western church has been seeing the world in black and white for some time, but we don't even realize it, not unlike the characters in *The Giver*. This has been caused by us forming Jesus in our own image rather than letting Jesus form us in his image. We have domesticated, Westernized, neutered, and altogether changed Jesus to an eternal Mr. Potato Head—ripping off the parts we don't like and adding what we think seems right.

Recently, in my own study and journey with Jesus and the Scriptures, I started to realize there are certain things about the first-century world that make Jesus and the Scriptures more vibrant, beautiful, and compelling. When you understand his world, you begin to understand him. There are things that make no sense to us because we don't know what it was like to be a first-century rabbi or a Jew living in Judea under Roman rule.

But when we enter into the world of Jesus, and take him for who he was, the Bible begins to turn to color. Details we haven't noticed before jump out at us. Neither the Bible nor Jesus change; but stepping back into the first century gives us new eyes to see who he was, what he did, and why we are still talking about him today.

I hope through these pages you might begin to see Jesus more vibrantly yourself. I'm not a pastor or theologian, and I don't have numerous degrees where people need to call me Doctor or

Professor Bethke. But over the past couple of years I've fallen more in love with Jesus and the story of God and his church by unclicking the mute button twenty-first-century Westerners have put on first-century Jesus and letting him speak on his own.

Every morning as I walk with Jesus, I ask him to open our eyes more and more each day. Because when we see Jesus clearly, then we can follow him.

One of the scariest questions we have to ask ourselves is, what if we aren't seeing Jesus properly? What implication does that have for our lives? What if Jesus isn't who we think? I believe he's always catching us off guard, creatively challenging us, pursuing us, and loving us.

I've written these pages as someone who—like you—is on a journey to see Jesus more vibrant, alive, and for who he truly is more and more each day. Will you join me?

CHAPTER ONE

YOUR STORY'S NOT WHAT YOU THINK

LOVE DEFINED YOU BEFORE ANYTHING ELSE DID

CHRISTIANITY IS A BOUNCED CHECK TO MY GENERATION.
We heard the promises, the value of "coming to Jesus"—
payouts such as a better life and no more problems—but when
we went to cash in on those promises, nothing deposited. The
investment didn't deliver what it said it would deliver. So we put
our trust into things that did (or at least felt like it).

I still remember when I first started truly following Jesus my
freshman year of college and began to go to church with a whole
new perspective. I wanted to learn more about Jesus, but I found
myself dreading going every week. The church I was attending
frequently put the perfect, shiny-rainbow Jesus follower onstage,
who made me feel even worse. Half the time I was expecting an
angel to fly over the stage with Handel's *Messiah* playing from the
clouds.

During what was called "testimony time," someone would be
invited to share for a few minutes about his or her life before and
after Jesus. Usually they'd say something like, "I was an alcoholic
for forty years and struggled every day with no hope. I gave my
life to Jesus and have never thought about a drop since."

While many people have that type of story, I don't. So every time I'd hear testimonies like that, I'd sink deeper into my chair and look around, wondering if anyone felt the same. Was I the only one who didn't have that kind of experience?[1] Was there something wrong with me? Did God not love me? Did I mess up and not become "Christian" enough?

Because when I started following Jesus, things actually got harder. I had a long season of depression. Things in my life started to go poorly. Relationships broke. Addictions stayed. I knew I didn't want to live for myself, or listen to the fleshy desires in me, but they still called me and lured me more. I felt I had no place in Christianity.

When I was a kid, the Christianity I saw never really gave much space to struggle, fail, or ask for help. Growing up in the '90s and coming of age in the beginning of the twenty-first century was a really peculiar place to be. It's as if we are in the middle of that monumental shift from Christianity being the law of the land to now becoming adamantly opposed. How'd we get here?

Western Christianity today is a weird stew of some biblical teachings and some gnostic principles, in a heavy modern enlightenment foundation with a Jesus sticker slapped on it. And sadly that combination leads to erosion, decay, and a Christianity that is honestly neither fulfilling nor enticing. In fact, it's pretty lifeless. It's not a compelling story because it's usually not a story at all. It's a formula, or facts, or a math equation.

But what if there is a better way? I truly believe Jesus tells a better story.

In order for Christianity to start fresh, we have to start with the gospel.

My first memorable encounter with the gospel was when I was in middle school. All around me other middle school kids were crying and hardly anyone was standing. It was a powerful moment—so much so that even now when I think about it, a range of emotions comes over me.

I was at a Christian youth camp.

It was the last night of that camp when everyone "asked Jesus into their hearts." The piano was playing softly while the camp speaker asked all the kids to bow their heads and close their eyes. He would then say, "Okay, whoever wants to receive Jesus, repeat after me. . . ."

Sound familiar? Welcome to 1990s evangelicalism.

Considering how common that experience was for people back then, there's something that has always struck me: *Why is it that a similar situation, when read as if it were part of the gospel narrative, feels weird or off base?*

Imagine you pick up the Gospel of Luke, and you see a bunch of red letters (the words of Jesus). You start reading those red letters, and it says, "All righty, everyone, bow your heads and close your eyes. The worship leader is going to come play some soft piano music behind me, and if you think you want to follow me, just put your hand in the sky. Don't worry: no one is looking." And when someone raises his hand, Jesus says, "I see your hand; God sees your heart."

It's almost comical, isn't it? Jesus' exhortations to his listeners were almost exactly the opposite. His declaration to follow him bled grace—to the point of bleeding himself—but in that grace he said, *"Follow me."* The abandon, the unknown, the reference to a first-century torture device, all crashed into that two-word phrase, *follow me*. We privatize our faith, when Jesus calls us to follow him publicly.

How did we get so far off base? How come our gospel doesn't really seem much like Jesus' gospel?

Here's a scarier question: at what point is a religion only wrong in a few areas but still the same belief system, and at what point is a religion so unrecognizable to its founders they'd call it a different religion entirely? Have we reached that point in Western Christianity?

I can't help but look at the Scriptures and the Christianity I've lived and breathed most of my life and think, *Really? Is this it? What happened?* The truth is, we are living in a really, really bad story. And a lot of us are not only living in it, but telling others, "If you come to Jesus, you can escape this world." (Yet didn't Jesus say he came to restore this world?)

When I was a kid, this thing called *heaven* was always spoken of as somewhere far away up in the sky. I always imagined heaven being a place far, far away with winged babies playing harps and floating on the clouds. Now honestly, that doesn't sound like a place where I want to be for eternity. It sounds terrible and boring. In fact, if I ever saw a naked chubby baby with wings, I'd probably run as fast as I could the other way; I wouldn't say, "Oh, I sure want to go there when I die." What if there's *better* news than the good news that Christians are going to heaven when we die? What if God wants to give us heaven right here? In our families? Our jobs? Our meals? Our art?

Another bad story a lot of Christians live in is what I call

"Cliffs Notes Christianity." It usually begins the story with Jesus: Jesus came to show you your sin, die for your sin, resurrect, and float off into heaven. It's a sterile, clean, plastic Jesus. It's the Christianity of show. It's nice, tidy—a neat package with a perfect bow on it. But walking with Jesus is way messier than that, like all of life truly is.

The problem with a CliffsNotes faith is we are disregarding the very story Jesus himself believed and lived! It starts with the New Testament and leaves out the fact that Jesus himself only had Genesis to Malachi as his Bible (or his story).

Many of us, without knowing it, rip Jesus' Jewishness right out of the story. But it's his Jewishness that informs the gospels and the story of Jesus himself. Jesus was a Jew and a rabbi. He probably had the Torah (first five books of the Bible) memorized, if not the entire Tanakh (Old Testament). The Old Testament is a lengthy, weaving, extensive collection of texts that seem to end without delivering what they all call for—a Messiah. A lot of us often skip from Genesis right to Matthew, leaving Israel's story in the dust. There's a reason Jesus didn't come in Genesis 4, but instead in Matthew 1. Jesus is the climax of the story, not the introduction.

If you can tell the gospel—or the story—of Jesus without even mentioning the story of Israel, it's probably not really the gospel, or at least not a full one.

So what story are you walking in? What's the plot? Who's the main character? What's the goal?

We all have answers to those questions whether or not we know them. To many Westerners, the plot is that life has no meaning and so you may as well enjoy it while you can. The main character is myself. And the goal is to enjoy it—gain as much as possible, as easily as possible, with as little pain as possible. When I was in college, this was basically the story every one of my friends was living in.

Others live in a story that is driving toward Utopia. It's about continuing out of primitive religions, philosophies, and ideas, and making the world a better place one step at a time. Sadly, they don't realize that the most "advanced" full century we've ever lived in, the twentieth century, is also on record as the bloodiest. It seems enlightenment of ideas and philosophy aren't going to achieve a utopia.

So what's the true story? Which is the best story?

The truth is, Christians have the greatest story ever told, but we aren't telling it.

The crucial left turn Christians often make when telling our story starts with the first three chapters of the very first book in the Bible—Genesis.

Genesis is a deeply beautiful, poetic, rhythmic, powerful book. *"In the beginning . . ."*

Quite a start, right? Not, "Let me tell you some facts, theories, and abstract truths," but, "Let me tell you a *story*."

Yet as Christians we often miss what's going on in the very first chapters of the very first book of the Bible. Many Christians don't even read Genesis 1–2 unless they need an offensive weapon against evolutionists. Because of this, many start their functional Bible in Genesis 3, especially when presenting the good news of Jesus.

This is evident in the "gospel bracelet" that has six different colors to help navigate the American gospel story. (And I say "American" because it breaks down the gospel in a Western, modern, abstract truth way that would have been foreign to Jesus.) The problem with those bracelets, though, is most of them start with the color *black*. If you've ever seen one, the order they usually take is similar to below.

- Black for sin
- Red for blood
- Blue for baptism
- White for cleansing
- Green for growth
- Yellow for heaven

I used to wear one of these bracelets and could "take people through it" like they were on some type of assembly line.[2] But there's something strange about those six steps. I'd contend that this "gospel" is a large reason for much of the distortion, malnutrition, condemnation, and lack of true healing and freedom in the church today.

The problem is, it starts with black. The bracelet's story *starts* with sin. That's like trying to build a house on rot. We want to tell people Jesus is the best thing ever, and the first thing we tell them is they are horrible and sinful and wretched. We are literally training people to start the "good news" with horrendously terrible news: "Hi, my name is Jeff. Can I talk to you for a second? You are a sinner."

Some of you might ask, "What's the problem? Isn't it true?"

Yes, it's true, we are broken, but even though it's true, it doesn't mean that's where God *starts* the story.

Starting the story with sin is like starting *The Chronicles of Narnia* with Edmund's capture by the White Witch. Or imagine the first page of *Where the Wild Things Are* already has Max in the jungle environment with the beasts. You probably wouldn't even know he was dreaming! Where you start a story drastically changes how you perceive that story.

Stories have a flow and an arc, a beginning and an end. When reading an encyclopedia or a dictionary, we can flip to any spot and get information, but when reading a story, we need to follow the narrative.

So if Genesis doesn't start in Genesis 3, why would we start there when telling it?

My point is this: black represents Genesis 3. It represents the point in the human story when we stage a coup d'état on God's throne and have been doing so ever since.

It's as if we're saying, "You're not God; I am. You don't know what's right and wrong; I do. I know you've given me the very oxygen in my lungs that allows me to live, but step aside. I can take it from here."

When we begin with sin, we feel spiritually and emotionally naked. Shame, guilt, and condemnation distort our beings at the truest level. Things don't work how they are supposed to work. We know something is broken, amiss.

But that's not where the story starts.

Any reading of ancient Jewish thought would show the first two chapters of Genesis were critical to their worldview and to

Jesus'. These were the chapters that concreted their very radical notion of monotheism, which was and still is a pillar of Jewish thought—one God over all creation, as opposed to many other societies at the time of ancient Israel who believed in regional gods of the sun, moon, and crops, among others.

And the first couple of chapters of Genesis are beautifully written. God makes order, beauty, and meaning out of chaos. Before God touched his finger to creation, it says it was *tohu va bohu*, which literally means "void and empty." But God starts making stuff, starts bringing beauty.

If you've ever seen a painter at work in his studio or a carpenter making something beautiful out of the best cuts of wood there are, you can only imagine the scene when God created *everything*.

And he just won't stop. Animals, stars, flowers, water, and land. And then, as the crowning act of creation, he makes two image-bearers—male and female—and puts them into the garden to reflect, cultivate, and steward. He points them to the cultivated part of the garden where everything has been made right and tells them to make the rest of the world look like that.

Talk about a story! The joy, elation, and mystery to be there in the beginning. Purpose, love, marriage, intimacy—it's all there.

So the question arises, why don't we start there? Why not tell that story?

Are you a Genesis 1 Christian or a Genesis 3 Christian?

Do you start your story with *shalom* or with sin?

Shalom is the Hebrew word for "peace." For rhythm. For everything lining up exactly how it was meant to line up.

Shalom is happening in those moments when you are at the dinner table for hours with good friends, good food, and good wine.

Shalom is when you hear or see something and can't quite explain it, but you know it's calling and stirring something deep inside of you.

Shalom is a sunset, that sense of exhaustion yet satisfaction from a hard day's work, creating art that is bigger than itself.

Shalom is enemies being reconciled by love.

Shalom is when you are dancing to the rhythm of God's voice.

And in Genesis 1, *everything* was shalom. It was shouting out of every square inch of the creation and exploding in every molecule in God's good earth. It was a crashingly loud symphony coming through the best surround-sound system you've ever encountered, hitting you from all angles at the peak of intensity. Yet now it's a dying whisper, a fractured song, a broken melody, only brought back into the right key at the feet of Jesus.

Genesis 1 Christians start the story with an appeal to the fact that all human beings on earth have inherent worth and value because they were brought to life by God's very own breath. They are living creatures standing in the gap between Creator and the rest of creation. All of creation God *spoke* into existence, but with us it said we were *formed*.

God got particular and creative with us human creatures. He rolled up his sleeves when he made us and declared us to be *Imago Dei. Image of God*. He did not call us broken, sinner, or failure.[3] Which means our *primal* identity (the one most at the depths of who we are—in our very bones) is one given by the Creator himself. We are his.

While it is true that after Genesis 3 we are sinners, we are still made in the image of God, no matter how broken that image is. Beauty is more primal than the curse; and we were children before we were runaways.[4]

Think about it: when a temple gets destroyed, and there is just rubble and remains on the ground, it is still a temple. A broken, cracked, messed up temple, yes, but it's still a temple. Its primal identity doesn't change. It didn't magically turn into an apartment building or a deli when it crumbled. It's a broken temple that has no hope of fixing itself and is in need of massive restoration from the ground up—but it's still a temple. So it is with us. When we start in Genesis 1, we tell a story that is more beautiful and much bigger than most Christians today tell, a story that needs to be heard by the world. We don't have a hard time realizing how messed up we are. I know I'm broken. I know I'm deeply flawed. I know I'm not good enough. You don't need to shout those things out at me from the corner of the street with your sandwich board—*I already know them.*

But you tell me I have inherent worth and value based on who made me, not what I do and I think, *Really? Are you sure? But . . .*

That's subversive. In a culture that continually strips humans of dignity (homelessness, exploitation of poor, objectifying women, abortion, euthanasia, and so forth), we have to return to *shalom.* We have to return to that special declaration God shouted over humans thousands of years ago in that wonderful garden—"So God created man in his *own* image."[5]

It doesn't matter how hard you scrub, in this life you can't get the image of God fully off of you.

Now from a personal to cosmic level, there is another vital distinction in making sure you start where God starts the story. When you start the story in Genesis 3, personal sin is the biggest problem in the world. Sin management is the problem and Jesus arrives simply to pay for your sin.[6]

The world doesn't matter. Creation doesn't matter. Only we matter because in Genesis 3 the story zooms in on the human condition. Now is that true? Of course, but it's not *all* of the truth. When you start in Genesis 1, you start with shalom not just of humans but of all creation. When God created the world it had perfect peace. There was this beautiful dance that the trees, the animals, the water, the sun, the rhythms of life, and the living creatures Adam and Eve were all doing. No one missed a step.

But when sin came into the world it fractured that dance, broke the rhythm, stopped the symphony. Creation stopped playing Beethoven's symphonies and started sounding more like sixth-grade me trying to learn my first note on the trombone. My mom didn't say, *"Oh, that's so beautiful."* She probably plugged her ears most of the time. It was *off.* And broken.

But when you start with the creation of all things as good because that's exactly what God said about them (food, music, relationships, beauty, and all of heaven and earth being flooded with God's presence), then the answer instead isn't sin management but restoration of all things. God is putting his world back together, and to do that he's using the very people who broke it.

The level of reconciliation and restoration goes way deeper.

God is recreating and remaking *everything* in the person and work of Jesus, and you can only get that when you get he cares about all that in the first place (Genesis 1–2). Jesus declared a new world was bursting forth right here in the midst of the old one, and you can't get that unless you know the whole world needs restoring. Some people say this way of explaining and understanding the gospel message is taking sin lightly, but I'd argue the exact opposite. What makes sin bigger? Humans being affected by it, or the whole world (including humans) being affected by it? And when sin is that big, it makes what Jesus accomplished even bigger.

How we understand this comes back to how we see the Bible. If we don't see it as a narrative, we won't tell it as one. And if we don't believe God loves us for who we are even before we ask to be forgiven, then we won't really even care to hear—let alone believe—his words.

HOW YOU SEE THE BIBLE SHAPES YOUR VIEW OF GOD

One of my favorite things my sweet wife, Alyssa, does began before we were married. Whenever I go on a trip, she writes me notes of encouragement, one for every day I'm gone. I hardly make it to the airport before opening *all of them* all at once.

I can't help myself. They bring me so much joy, life, and encouragement that I want to read them all in one sitting. (I was also that kid who begged my parents to let me open my presents two weeks before Christmas. Patience is obviously a virtue I hold innately.) I'm so antsy to read them all because I truly believe

Alyssa loves me, is all for my joy, encourages me, and cares about me. If this weren't the case, I wouldn't be tempted to read them. We are more inclined to read someone's words when we believe those words are there because they care for us.

Do you really believe God loves you? Admittedly, the word *love* is a little fuzzy and overused in our culture. How about, do you believe God *likes* you? Delights in you? Knows you? Dances because of you? Because if you do, then I have a feeling that motivation to pick up his grand narrative called the Bible won't be that big of a problem.

I've seen a lot of books or blogs on how to study or read the Bible. You can use all the techniques in the world, but if you think God is burdened by you, is aloof, or doesn't care about you, then you'll be predisposed to have a distorted lens through which you view him right from the beginning.

So what lens do you see the Bible through? A road map to life? A sword? A collection of stories? Even though you probably don't think so, the answer to that question has cosmic implications. Your answer to that question ultimately gives you a very specific view of God and your role as someone under him.

For example, a common metaphor in the Christian world is that the Bible is the "sword of the Spirit." The writer of Ephesians (6:17) uses the imagery of a sword to explain God's word has an edge to it; it's sharp and can create things. It can cut deep. It has power. It divides between soul and spirit, bone and marrow.

But if you see the Scriptures only as a "sword," it says something very specific about God. It projects that he is nothing more than a sergeant or captain who has commissioned us to fight in a war. And if God is a captain of an army, then that makes us soldiers. Of course sword imagery is used in the Scriptures, but it's not the ultimate narrative. We don't see it in creation, the history of Israel, or the words of Jesus.

In fact, it's only used on a few occasions to convey a special aspect of the Christian life. So it's a subnarrative (meaning it's true, and it's there), but it's an illustration used to serve a greater narrative. The word *soldier* isn't used nearly as often as *bride* or *child*. When elevated to the level of the ultimate theme of the Bible, elevating subnarratives to a primary status can distort the truth and create those groups of people you see wielding their "swords," quoting verses about "those" evil people, and creating an us-versus-them culture.

Another lens some people use is seeing the Bible as a moral compass listing precepts we should follow. The problem with that is a lot of parts of the Bible are certainly things we don't want to follow. There is murder, adultery, rape, incest, and a whole slew of terrible things. One way I heard a pastor say it that helps me, is that the Bible is *descriptive* not *prescriptive*. It's mainly about how God relates to a broken and rebellious human race, and in the midst of that narrative he gives some precepts and ways to live.

Still others view the Bible as nothing more than a road map for life. Of course the Bible does contain some specific guidelines; Proverbs is nothing but advice given to the young as they embark on the world. But we have to admit the Bible is not the user-friendly manual we would choose. It doesn't tell us what colleges to attend, what person to marry, or what jobs to take. It does have razor-sharp focus on God's ultimate will being that we follow him, live humbly, seek justice, and be obedient.

When you view the Bible as your personal road map, you can't help but create a God who is a blend of Santa Claus and the magic eight ball. He exists to satisfy your desires, answer your specific questions, and give you exact details about who he wants you to marry or what school he wants you to go to. This view of the Bible places you as the center of the story. The world is revolving around you, and God is present as butler, not Lord.

There are plenty of examples of the Bible through different lenses. And while each view isn't completely wrong as a subnarrative, the problem comes when we often give those distortions the ultimate importance rather than seeing them as simply pieces of the pie.

Remember, the Bible is sixty-six books and letters, written by almost forty different authors, and spanning more than thirty-five hundred years. Among the authors are kings, prophets, apostles, and shepherds. Imagine one letter written by President John F. Kennedy and another letter written by a fifth-century peasant. There would be enormous differences in the cultural, sociological, and philosophical frameworks they were operating in. And that's the beauty of the Scriptures. It's full of songs, histories, genealogies, and letters that have brought hope to millions down the ages, written from many different perspectives, different lenses, different subnarratives.

With that in mind, the best way to view Scripture as a whole is as a *story*—a long story that is full of the bumps and bruises, twists and turns, plotlines, character development, climaxes, and conclusions every story should have. The narrative thread that ties these diverse texts together is God's rescue operation of this thing called humanity. The creation account, the Law, the Prophets, the songs, the Gospels, the Epistles, and the book of Revelation all tell the same story—how the Creator God (Jesus) brought about (and is still bringing about) new creations despite our rebellion, sin, and cosmic treason.

The Bible is about God—specifically about how God became King of the world. In Genesis, God created us so he could dwell with us and be our God. In the Old Testament, the mission of God *dwelling* with us is central.

- The Old Testament is all about what it will ultimately look like when God becomes King and restores this world.
- The Gospels are about what it looks like when God actually becomes King.
- The Epistles are about how to live in light of God being King.
- And Revelation is about the finality or conclusion where God is King and everything is in shalom as he intended in the first place.

And when we view the Scriptures as a story—more important, this specific story—we see our own roles *in* the story. We aren't at the center. We aren't on the main stage. The spotlight isn't on us. God created us to co-create with him. To co-labor in the task he commissioned to us. We aren't the story, but we are *in* the story!

THE GRAND NARRATIVE WITH GOD AT THE CENTER

Ultimately the Bible isn't about us, and that's good news.

Have you ever gone to a movie just to watch the extras? No one does that. Personally, I go to any movie Denzel Washington or Will Smith is in. I don't care what it's about. If one of them is in it, I see it.

But imagine watching one of Denzel's movies when, during a close-up of his face, you see something strange in the background. You squint because it's fuzzy and blurry. Soon, though, it becomes obvious it's an extra in the movie, flailing his arms, trying to distract from the scene. The extra wants the spotlight. That would be incredibly weird.

That doesn't ever happen because the movie is about Denzel's character (and that scene wouldn't make it past the final edit). When the extra plays his small role well, acting as a tool pointing moviegoers toward the main story (which, if he does his job properly he goes unnoticed), then the film flows perfectly.

That's us with God. We are in *his* story, his redemption and rescue operation. He is King. He is Lord. He is on the throne. And when we live our lives pointing to ourselves, we look just as stupid as an extra in the background flailing his arms during his three-second spot on camera.

We need to make sure we read the Bible as a *story*. After all, it's the greatest story ever told. It's the reason we all feel a whisper in our hearts every time we read a good story. It's a signpost point-ing to the one all of us are in. A wonderful kingdom narrative with God at the center.

But, in Christianity, oftentimes, we tell a really bad story like the static testimonies onstage I mentioned in the beginning of this chapter ("I was bad, I found Jesus, now my life is perfect."). Or we don't tell a story at all. We tell facts. Facts devoid of story. Devoid of life. Devoid of personality.

But the truth is story is the language and currency of the world.

Don't believe me? Try to remember highlights from the last sermon you heard, then try to remember the premise of the last movie you saw. My guess is the latter is best remembered. Sadly, today's sermons often aren't a beautiful art of storytelling like they used to be; rather, they are encyclopedic regurgitations of facts devoid of skin. That type of language doesn't sink in, doesn't resonate, doesn't make our heart beat. A good movie, on the other hand, can draw you into another life and take you places.

When someone recites, "Fourscore and seven years ago our fathers brought forth on this continent, a new nation," most Americans immediately recognize the Gettysburg Address. In one of the most famous speeches of all time, Abraham Lincoln, in just fifteen words, started to tell a story. About our nation. Our history. Characters, timeline, plot, and problem—they're all there. And it deeply strikes us.

One of my favorite movies is *Amistad*. It's an incredibly gritty and raw look at slavery and Western imperialism. In one scene President John Quincy Adams is asked for advice in regards to the court case defense. Adams says, "When I was an attorney, a long time ago, . . . I realized, after much trial and error, that in the courtroom, *whoever tells the best story wins.*"[7]

If we want our neighbors, our coworkers, and our family to think about Jesus differently, it's time we start telling a better story. *Whoever tells the best story wins.* As theologian N. T. Wright put it,

> Most Western churches have simply forgotten what the Gospel message is all about, and what the Bible, seen as a whole, is all about: that this is the story of how the Creator God launched his rescue operation for the whole of creation. As a result, the great narrative the Bible offers has been shrunk, by generations of devout preachers and teachers, to the much smaller narrative of "me and God getting together," as though the whole thing—creation, Abraham, Moses, David, the early church, and not least the Gospel themselves—were simply a gigantic set of apparent authorities teaching about how unbelievers come to faith, how sinners get saved, and how people's lives get turned around. Of course, the Bible includes plenty about all that, but it includes within the much larger story of creation and cosmos, covenant God and covenant people—the single narrative that, according to all four gospels, reaches its climax with Jesus.[8]

We are trained to rip the story right out and are left with a skeleton of facts and truths that have no personal connection. There is something innate in the Western mind-set that gravitates much more toward assembly line information rather than creativity and beauty.

Sir Ken Robinson, an expert on education reform, describes how we are training ourselves to abandon story and creativity. Writing about divergent thinking (the ability to think of multiple possibilities out of the box), he notes a famous study where he gives kindergarten students one paper clip each and asks them to think of as many uses for it as they can. The study was re-administered to the same kids every three to five years until they graduated from high school.

Of the fifteen hundred students, how many scored at the genius level for divergent thinking as kindergarteners? Ninety-eight percent.

Every time the test was re-administered, the percentage of geniuses dropped. This is fascinating. You'd think children would improve at problem solving and innovation, especially in an educational system. "But one of the most important things happened that I'm convinced [sic] is that by now they've become educated. They spend ten years in school being told there is one answer, it's at the back, and don't look—and don't copy because that's cheating."[9]

I can't help but think of some church circles. We don't realize our industrial revolution and assembly-line mentality has crept into the church, virtually stealing people's creativity and sense of wonder. We go around saying, "You need to be born again." And to the next person: "You need to be born again." And to the next person: "Yeah, you also need to be born again." We industrialize and assembly line salvation. Just give me the formula!

But guess what? Jesus doesn't like formulas. Even that phrase *born again* was only mentioned once by Jesus in Scripture.[10]

In the very next story in John, Jesus tells a woman she needs to drink of the fount of living water and stop trying to satisfy her thirst other places.

Jesus was creative and made a habit of meeting people right where they were. Like a doctor, he prescribed exactly what was needed in that moment. By the way, the first story was a religious man who thought he was "good to go" because he had been *born* into the family of Abraham. In the next story, Jesus sat at a well and explained to a woman that well water doesn't satisfy an eternal thirst.

What if we taught people to eat, drink, and breathe the story of the Scriptures? To see their own stories within the big story? To tell a better story than the world's narrative?

The fascinating thing is that there is some good science to show this is how God meant for us to learn truth, in story.

A recent study showed that the right-brain hemisphere—the one that controls creativity, story, and art—is wired and designed to receive and compute information before the left-brain hemisphere—the logical side that controls analysis and understanding. Meaning, we were created to take in the big picture and engage on all senses through art and beauty before we go hash it all out.

Instead, letting our left brains take the lead, according to N. T. Wright, is the "cultural equivalent of schizophrenia. But these assumptions run deep in today's world, and they have radically conditioned the way we approach everything, including not least the Bible."[11]

No wonder Jesus didn't have his disciples sit down at desks, with him at the whiteboard.

Jesus' followers walked with him. And while they walked, he told stories—stories of sheep, lost coins, wedding banquets, different types of soils, a rich man and a poor man, two lost sons, someone coming knocking at midnight, and so on.

Jesus is the most creative, dynamic, and alluring teacher to ever walk this earth, and we relegate him to the mantle of our fireplace. No one's words explode with more power and draw out more wonder and awe than those of this first-century man from Nazareth, yet we prefer to give someone four spiritual laws or the Romans Road.[12]

It's about time we stop with the formulas and start with the truth and beauty of story.

We have the greatest story ever told, so let's start living in it and let's start telling it.

CHAPTER TWO

THE TEMPLE'S NOT WHAT YOU THINK

IT'S GOD PITCHING HIS TENT IN YOUR BACKYARD

WHEN I WAS GROWING UP, I THOUGHT TATTOOS WERE A BAD thing. Meaning, Jesus died for people who have tattoos. Tattoos were a sin. Usually people would justify this viewpoint by quoting part of 1 Corinthians 6:19: *"Your body is a temple of the Holy Spirit."*

The way they used it, that verse could just as easily justify preaching against fast food since all those artificial ingredients are also destructive to your body. When you read that sentence in its context, however, you learn that Paul was writing specifically about sins you *can't* see, namely the mysterious union of human sexuality.

What if, however, that verse on our bodies being temples was far more explosive, cataclysmic, and downright scandalous than we thought?

In first-century Judea the word *temple* held plenty of weight and was incredibly charged. It appeared on almost every page of the Hebrew Scriptures and was the center of the Jewish lifestyle. We misunderstand the connotation of *temple* because we don't have literal temples or use that word much anymore (well, technically we do have them: we just call them malls, stadiums, and banks).

A temple is a place of worship, and in Paul's and Jesus' world, it specifically was the place where heaven and earth met. As if heaven and earth were two separate circles, and the circles overlap in the middle, and they called that place the temple.[1]

Heaven was seen as God's dimension. The place where he dwelled. Where everything he decreed was happening exactly how he wanted. Heaven operates in shalom. And the Jewish people before Jesus saw the temple as that space ripped down here onto earth. Once they entered the temple, they were entering the space where human space collided with God's.

But to really understand the significance of the temple, we have to go back to the beginning. Many Christians were raised on Genesis 1 and 2 being a battleground instead of a beautiful narrative. When these two chapters are mentioned, many people immediately want to jump to the debate about the details of the creation of days.

When I was growing up, Genesis 1 was the soil in which you proved if you were a good Christian or not. It was a litmus test. Was the world created in seven days, or is evolution true? Is the earth six thousand years old or 4.5 billion years old?

The basic problem with *both* of those thought lines is, we are looking in a book for an answer it doesn't give. Expecting Genesis 1 to prove the world is or isn't six thousand years old is like asking Shakespeare to prove that gravity exists or that the earth revolves around the sun. The simple truth is that Shakespeare and the biblical authors didn't write their books to answer those questions. Might Christians have just a tad more humility and winsomeness when trying to prove things from Scripture that weren't even the original authors' intent?

Do we really think the author of Genesis was saying, "You know what? I really want people to believe the world was created in seven literal twenty-four-hour periods," as he told the creation story? Of course we can deduce that, but let's be honest and admit that wasn't his intent. Read in a full sweep, it's clear Genesis is not about the fine-tuned details, but about the big picture of beginnings. Genesis answers the why, not the how.

The book of Genesis was written after the Israelites left Egypt and wandered in the wilderness for a generation. Now remember, the Israelites had just come out of more than four hundred years of slavery, which included oppression, angst, and brutal conditions.

If firsthand accounts of slavery and abuse of antebellum African Americans make you cringe, this should too. The Egyptians were ruthless. They were bitter. They hated and feared that the Israelite birthrate was outpacing the Egyptian rate.

The Israelites endured "misery and suffering"[2] as Egypt had turned one of the very blessings and joy of the creation mandate, work, into one of the biggest tools of oppression and pain for the Israelites. They made bricks with no rest and endured beatings if the quota wasn't met. I'm sure, similar to many other times of harsh slavery in history, they were beaten and even sometimes killed at will, not seen as human, raped, verbally abused, and altogether crushed.

And when you are in conditions such as these you lose track of your story. You lose memory of who you are, why you're there, and where you came from. Moses told the stories in Genesis, along with the rest of the Torah, to remind Israel of why they were there, who their God was, and how his promises and plans went back to the very inception of the created order. Telling a really bad story—one that's filled with pain and oppression—would have left them confused and with no context for their wilderness struggles. They needed to hear a *better* story, a truer story.

Our little daughter, Kinsley, is six months old. Moses telling the stories of Genesis was like me telling our Bethke family stories to Kinsley. When she's a little older and we are down by the campfire, I'll share stories with her of our family, traditions, redemption, grace, and purpose.

She'll find out that her mother and I dated but then went through a pretty hard breakup before we got back together and eventually married. She'll find out why we decided to raise her on Maui where Alyssa lived for a couple of years while we were dating, instead of Seattle where both Alyssa and I were raised. She'll find out why she was named Kinsley and why I'll never let her get on a motorcycle. (My dad owned a Harley shop most of his life, and I saw him get in a few accidents that left him banged up and bruised.) I'll share with her the stories that led to her life. It's hard to know where you're going if you don't know where you've been.

That's what Genesis was and is. The Israelites had just come out of Egypt, but Egypt was still in them. The Egyptian way of living, the constant work, the idolatry—that's the only life these Israelites knew.

So Moses told them stories of their ancestors to prove that God is not like the gods in Egypt. That's not what he requires of us. That's not why we are here. They have a story before slavery. They have a purpose.

I can see kids huddled up around the campfire while the

parents told their kids these epic stories of the garden, of Abraham, Joseph, and more. When you zoom back and do a quick fly-over of Genesis, you see it really has two parts. Before chapter 11 all the stories are about the downward spiral: Cain kills his brother. The wickedness of the entire world. The tower of Babel where humanity wants to make "a name for themselves."

And then all of a sudden chapter 12 makes a 180-degree turn: God tells a Mesopotamian trader named Abram he is going to rescue the entire world through his family line. Chapters 12–50 are the epic drama following that promise through the lives of Abraham, Isaac, Jacob, and Joseph as they sometimes thwart but never lose that blessing. God is faithful.

But let's focus on the very beginning: in the first chapter of Genesis, we see this incredible, beautiful telling of the creation of the world. Within the first three verses we meet a God who is Spirit, a God who speaks, and a God who is Creator all in one divine being. One who makes order and beauty out of chaos. Who creates space, and then fills that space with beauty.

Have you ever watched a suspenseful or mind-bending movie—some of my favorites include *Inception* and *The Sixth Sense*—that make much more sense the second time around? You watch it again, and you see things that make lightbulbs go off that you didn't even come close to noticing the first time?

The book of Genesis is like that. The ancient Near Eastern world was very different from our own, and the authors wrote assuming their readers had the same cultural memory they did. Modern readers, such as you and me, have different cultural memories. We don't even come close to seeing all the metaphors and references in Genesis because we are so far removed from that culture.

If an ancient Near Eastern scribe had picked up Genesis 1–2, he would have recognized it as a *temple-building* text. Ancient Hebrews would have seen many markers in Genesis 1 and 2 that point to something we miss. Similar to texts of the time, it followed a structure that texts only followed when writing about a temple being built. All temple-building texts had two huge markers to distinguish themselves from other literature.

The first thing to recognize is all temples, when they would be completed, would put the image of that god in the temple on the last day as a sort of seal or marking that it was done. The second thing would be the builders would rest and celebrate the day after they had finished, and formally invite the god to take up residence. It was an ancient version of an inauguration ceremony. It'd be seen as a day of rest where you'd invite the god to flood the temple with his presence.

Sound familiar?

In Genesis 1–2, on the last day of creation, God the builder (1) places Adam and Eve in the garden as his image-bearers, and (2) rests from his work, makes that day the Sabbath as a remembrance, and enters the garden himself. Hebrew and Israelite listeners and readers would have recognized those markers and said, "God is following temple-building patterns in the telling of the story." Genesis is all about a temple being built.

But the strange thing about this text that is completely unique and different to other ancient Near Eastern religions is that there's no building. No tabernacle. No brick and mortar. No temple.

Image-bearers always go in or on a temple. And they can't move. They are metal, wood, stone, etc. But in Genesis the images are flesh. A divine mix of spirit, flesh, love, and humanness. And Adam and Eve are placed in the garden, which is God saying loud and clear that from the beginning he wants to flood the earth with his presence. The whole world is his temple.

On day seven God flooded the earth with his presence. While other gods were regional and controlled only particular elements of nature such as the sun or sea or field, this God of Israel was God of *all* and God of *everywhere*. The ancient Near East sees gods a lot like how we see chief leaders of states.

It's totally fine and warranted to think the prime minister of Israel is prime minister in Israel, but not in China. And the president of the United States is exactly that: the president of only the fifty United States. But what happens if someone starts saying the president of the United States is actually president over every person and country in the world? That would upset a lot of people. It's not so subtly calling all the other leaders parodies or fake powers.

That's exactly what Scripture is claiming of God. He is God of everything, everywhere, all the time. And he's not a ruthless, fickle, borderline-schizophrenic God like the rest. Most ancient Near East gods constantly had to be appeased to keep the sun rising and the seas flowing and the crops growing. And if something was going wrong, you had to scramble quickly to find out what god you upset.

But the true God over the whole world is a God of beauty. Of wonder. Of love. He creates a space where his children can flourish, and he cares about his creation and his image-bearers.

Today, the second most widely known creation story is the *Enuma Elish*, a Babylonian poem that was imprinted on seven tablets around the seventeenth century BC. Marduk, who would become the chief of all Babylonian gods, creates humans to be the gods' minions. The making of humans is a side note to the rise of Marduk in this myth, yet in Genesis humanity is the climax of creation! We are God's image-bearers. We have a piece of him, are part of his likeness. He makes us co-creators and cultivators; then he sends us out into the world.

This was foundational to the Jewish story and deeply subversive after just coming out of Egypt, which treated them as slaves without worth.

In Exodus, God tells us that he "will dwell among the people of Israel and will be their God."[3] Millennia later, John, the writer of Revelation, tells us he "heard a loud voice from the throne saying, 'Behold, the dwelling place of God is with man. He will dwell with them, and they will be his people, and God himself will be with them as their God.'"[4] This is a major theme throughout Scripture.[5]

So one of the overarching themes in Scripture—from the very beginning to the very end—isn't to "get people saved" but for God to *dwell* down here with his people. We are so concerned about going up to heaven, but God is concerned with bringing heaven down to earth. Revelation 22 even says the new heavens and new earth won't need a temple because God will be our dwelling place (think back to Genesis!). We are working so hard to get out of this place, while God is working hard to recreate and come down to this place.

Because dwelling is God's goal, he provided instructions for building a tabernacle (think, *portable temple*) when he pulled the Israelites out of Egypt. God wanted to be in the midst of the Israelites. They were moving, so he would move with them.

Then later down the road, God gave Kings David and Solomon permission to and instructions for building a permanent dwelling place for him.[6]

The temple Solomon built, with God's glory in the Holy of Holies, came to represent the Israelites' national and personal identities. It was the center of everything: Jerusalem literally built up around it, and the people organized their lives according to its annual festivals. But Israel began to worship other gods. Maybe it was because they got tired of making frequent trips to Jerusalem, or maybe they just wanted perceived control over their own lives. Since the fall in Genesis 3 it was almost more natural to worship false gods rather than the real God.

The Israelites liked gods that were controllable, and the Creator God wasn't. They begin to make a mockery of the temple system. They wanted to pursue other gods around them, when the true God Yahweh was right in their midst. There's one point where some even begin following the god Molech who called for child sacrifice.

As judgment, and maybe as a sign to wake up them up, God sends the leaders of Jerusalem into exile in Babylon. They are enslaved to people who worship Marduk. The very presence of God is seen leaving the temple right before this judgment. And then the temple gets destroyed.[7]

Can you imagine how this must have felt? Imagine the White

House, the Pentagon, the Lincoln Memorial, the Washington Monument, and the Capitol were obliterated all at once. That's about as close as you can get to imagining what the Israelites felt when the temple complex was razed by the Babylonian emperor, Nebuchadnezzar. They would sing,

> *By the waters of Babylon,*
>   *there we sat down and wept,*
>   *when we remembered Zion.*
> *On the willows there*
>   *we hung up our lyres.*
> *For there our captors*
>   *required of us songs,*
> *and our tormentors, mirth, saying,*
>   *"Sing us one of the songs of Zion!"*[8]

They are undone.

A generation later, after Babylonia has been overthrown by Persia, some of the Jews are allowed to make their way back to Jerusalem and begin rebuilding the temple. But it's clear God isn't there anymore. The "shekinah glory," as it's called, never seems to return.

From this period, until the last sentence of the Old Testament, the Israelites are left wondering, when will God return to dwell with them? He promised he'd come back and be with his people. His very presence in their midst.

Can you imagine the hundreds of years of longing, aching, and praying for this to happen? With every year that passed, the expectation that God would do a new thing, a big thing, a monumental thing got larger and larger.

And then it happens. Just not the way they expected.

The Gospel of John, while the Jewish people are still waiting for the glory of Yahweh to return to his temple, says the first three words are

In the beginning.

Any faithful Jew would have immediately recognized the book's introduction as the same introduction to Genesis—the book of beginnings and creation, when God sealed the earth with his presence. John is invoking the Genesis language to get his readers ready for a new story about another beginning, or a new beginning, in the same way you'd know what I was invoking if I might start a speech with, "I have a dream, that one day."

Skip down a few verses from that first verse and we see one of our most famous Christmas verses. In the beginning there is this "Word" being, John says. And this Word being is somehow like God, with God, and is God. You've probably quoted John 1:14 right before sipping on hot chocolate and turning on Kenny G's Christmas album; it's a classic advent verse:

And the Word became flesh and dwelt among us.

But the Greek word translated as "dwelt" in that verse is *eskenosen*, which can literally mean "to fix a tent."

John is saying loud and clear that Jesus himself is pitching his tent (that is, his holy tabernacle) among us. His body is now the place where heaven and earth crash together. The temple system has reached its fulfillment and was always a signpost pointing to the great temple Jesus. The glory of God has returned to his temple, and it looks like a Jewish rabbi in Judea. How strange is that?

So John, in just a few verses, is purposely saying things to draw strong echoes. Jesus is the new genesis, the beginning of a new creation; and God himself is pitching his tent with us—*to be with his people.*

What if we believed that?

Growing up I believed that Jesus was very far away. That he was standing up in heaven with his arms crossed waiting for me to get it right. Or even if he did show me grace, I imagined it with rolling eyes saying, "Ugh, not the same mistake for the twenty thousandth time."

But John's words say otherwise. God really does want to dwell with me. He really wants to pitch his tent in my life. And when I continually fall, he says, "Hey, I'm in this for the long haul."

I often struggle with this concept because Jesus is a God who comes *close.* A God who is near, who we can touch, who can see our mess. A God who literally became one of us to achieve his goal.

You'd think the Jews would have said, "Yes! Finally! We've been waiting for this rescue to happen!"

But something peculiar happened: They *rejected* him. They said no thanks. He looked too strange. He was a baby. A peasant boy. A Nazarene. A rabbi who specifically said love, not violence, would take down evil. For hundreds of years the Jews were expecting a king who would come with a sword, defeat their oppressors, and restore the temple. They never expected their king was eating with drunks, sinners, and town prostitutes. How could this be the Messiah?

Israel's story, and how Jesus completely entered into that story but looked nothing like what people thought he would, is a lesson to us today too. Imagine you're going on a blind date with someone, but it will be fifty years from the time you set the date up to when you meet the person. For fifty years you are told he or she is a strong, tall warrior; and for fifty years you visualize what your date will be like. When you finally get to the restaurant, a scrawny, meek, and mild person comes in. You don't even consider that person because the reality is the opposite of your vision.

We should never put God in our preconceived box. We are made in his image, and it's dangerous when we reverse that and make God in our image. When we do, we miss his plans for us. With sorrow in his heart and the cross right in front of him, Jesus said, "You did not know the time of your visitation."[9] God walked right in front of the very people who were waiting for him, but they missed him.

The Gospel of Matthew records the life of Jesus for a Jewish audience. Just before his crucifixion, Jesus did some quirky things with a donkey, counting tables, and a fig tree. To understand just how shocking Jesus' actions were, we need to know some details of Israel's history.

You may have heard of King Ahab and his wife Jezebel. They were wicked monarchs in Northern Israel, and their son Joram was proving just as bad a ruler as his father had been. God sent his prophet Elisha to find Commander Jehu on a battlefield and anoint him king. When it was finished, Jehu's fellow soldiers spread their cloaks under his feet and chanted, "Jehu is king." (Jehu goes on to kill Joram with an arrow to his heart and trample the dead body of Jezebel—which is quite intense, but that's a story for another book.)[10]

So basically there was a current royalty and monarch in place, and Jehu completely and utterly upstages it, with the people showing they are in agreement of this move by placing the cloaks at his feet. This is a memorable story, so any first-century Jew would have recognized a parody of it. Jesus begins to enter Jerusalem. The capital. The epicenter. The place where the temple was—Zion.

This is Jesus' moment, and everyone knows it. The king is riding into the capital to take his rightful throne! But he does something incredibly strange: instead of riding in on a warhorse as Jehu would have, Jesus rides in on a donkey. Undeterred, most of the crowd spread their cloaks on the ground while screaming, "Hosanna! Son of David!" meaning, "Savior! King!"

Jesus is riding into the city giving his followers the parade they are asking for, just not in the way they are asking for it. They wanted someone to crush their Gentile rulers from Rome, but Jesus actually spoke harshest of Israel and Jerusalem itself.[11] They wanted a king, yet instead of a gold chair, Jesus would enthrone himself on a wooden Roman execution device below the most ironic sign in history: "King of the Jews." They were hoping that the Messiah would crush Rome and evil, but Jesus attacked the true enemies: sin and death.[12]

So what's the first thing Jesus is going to do after making such a bold and treasonous political statement? Start passing out weapons to stage an assault? Instead he makes a countercultural religious statement. He goes into the temple and flips the tables of the moneychangers.

This might be the most frequently misinterpreted passage in all Scripture. Growing up I always heard that Jesus flipping the tables was an indictment of people turning the temple into a business. Pimping out religion, per se. But that's how the temple system worked. Jews had to travel to Jerusalem to make their required sacrifices, and it was impractical to travel from Timbuktu with a posse of cows, sheep, and birds trailing behind you.

Animals (and grains and fruits and wines) were sold in the courtyard of the temple for the express purpose of sacrificing them to God. Jews would buy what they needed, then give the offering "ingredients" to a priest to sacrifice. This took money to do so. This was accepted tradition, and it wasn't what Jesus was critiquing. What offends him is much more insidious.

With a loud voice, I'm guessing, Jesus flips the tables and says, "My house shall be called a house of prayer, but you make it a den of robbers."[13] What Jesus does here is cook up a hybrid phrase from two very famous passages in the Old Testament that all his listeners that day in the temple would have known. One from Isaiah and the other from Jeremiah.

The full verse he quotes from Isaiah says: "for my house shall be called a house of prayer for all peoples." God intended that the temple would one day be a place where all nations and tribes would be welcome. Yet the temple had completely self-imploded. It had turned into a country club—a violent revolutionary country club at that.

The word *robbers* in Jesus' quotation may be translated "insurrectionists." The temple had become a stronghold for Jewish nationalists who were so zealous they believed they needed to incite violence to bring God's kingdom to earth. Israel and the temple existed to be the bearers of good news to the nations, and now Israel camped out and called all outsiders evil. And that's exactly what Jeremiah 7 is about—how evil and corrupt Israel had become.

There are a lot of rules in the Torah that make the temple available to only a certain type and group of people. It was exclusive because God was creating a family and a community to go out and bless the nations and be the light of the world. Yet Israel's light had gone out. They were focused on getting the Romans out of their lives instead of showing God to the empire.

Notice how the "lame and blind" came to Jesus as soon as he finished with the temple, and they found healing. The very people who were not allowed in the temple because their infirmities made them unclean were some of the first to benefit from Jesus, the true temple.

So Jesus rides in, and the first thing he does, rather than stick it to the Gentile enemies, is upend the temple and declare imminent judgment on his own people. Flipping the tables and chairs of the sacrifice-sellers was show theater, designed to be seen and to be disruptive. When all the money scattered on the floor, the sacrifices immediately stopped. When you can't buy a sacrifice, you can't sacrifice. And so in those brief moments, for however long it took to pick up all the coins and right the animal booths, the sacrificial system stopped.

It's no coincidence one of the first things he does after this public upheaval is curse a fig tree for bearing no fruit. A fig tree was a picture of Israel's leaders in the first century, and so he indicts the fig tree as an indictment of them. They have lost their way and the reason they existed. They are no longer a nation of priests that might welcome people into the family of God but instead have become violent revolutionaries that see everyone else as the enemy.

Then, as the mount of the temple stands right in the background, Jesus tells his disciples that when they trust in him they will have power to move these mountains. This wasn't about extraordinary power in prayer, even though that's true; it's Jesus giving his followers the strength and courage and reminder that, with him, an unlikely band of twelve people can go against one of the greatest religious institutions and symbols of all time, since it has lost its power and is now under judgment. The new place where God dwells is this band of misfits who live their life under the reign and rule of Jesus.

In our recent history, the beautiful Civil Rights Movement echoes this perfectly. What I love so much about Martin Luther King Jr. is that he never was advocating for something entirely new or different. He was just calling the leaders and institutions to stand true in accordance with the already enacted law, decrees, and constitution. Our forefathers made it clear all men were created equal, and the Civil Rights demonstrators stood while they were beaten, lynched, bitten by dogs, and firehosed, to say no, we will not back down.

An unlikely group can take down the powers that be—especially when the powers had turned corrupt. The very powers of the country that gave us all those rights had defaulted and gone defunct. They began to serve the very opposite purposes they were created to sustain—protect and provide for all people equally. And Jesus is still calling us to this high task today. Let us always be people who receive beauty, goodness, and grace from God only to reflect it out to our neighbors and world.

A GOD WHO IS VULNERABLE

Yesterday I did one of my favorite things: I got on the floor with our little girl, Kinsley, and basically made a fool of myself.

She can't walk yet, so we lay her on the floor with a few toys and watch her roll and tumble around the living room. I'll often hop down there with her and start rolling around on my stomach, laughing with her and just being on her level. I always talk to her in baby talk—you know, that language where you're saying nothing understandable and talking in a really high voice. I find it strange how normal that is, even though I clearly sound ridiculous.

When I jump down there with her, it's simply because I want to be with her. There's a special bond between a parent and a child, especially at that age, that isn't present between any other people.

Imagine I am going into a conference room for a business meeting, and upon entering I get down on the floor, rolling around and babbling. That would be weird, and the others would probably call the cops.

Baby talk is unique to my time with Kinsley, and in those moments I have no inhibitions. No holding back. Just simple childlike fun and love. And I love it. I'm not worrying about being efficient. I'm not worrying about saving face or making sure

Kinsley knows our proper roles. No, it's just me rolling up my sleeves and entering into her world.

I think the temple was like that. Sure, it was a lofty building, but in fact it's the very mode God has chosen to jump on our level and play with us.

There is a type of vulnerability to God coming in the temple. Whereas most gods have to be appeased and encouraged to stick around, the true God of the Scriptures puts a stake in the ground and stays. He says, "No, my goal is to dwell with my people, and I'm going to pursue them relentlessly until that happens." We may cringe at the idea of a vulnerable God, but a vulnerable God who is also all-knowing and all-powerful? That's a God I want to know.

Solomon's temple was an actual building. But we gloss over that without realizing that the very act of taking up residence in a building is an incredibly vulnerable and humble moment for the Creator. That means the infinite God put himself in the finite. The Creator of all things dwelled in wood and stone. You'd think the Israelites would have fallen on their feet and worshiped him because he chose to be with his people.

Nope. The indictments of Israel continue all throughout the prophets: stiff necked, idolatrous, ungrateful.

The amazing thing is that God doesn't snap his finger and say, "Fine. If you don't want me, then I don't want you." He certainly could have, but instead he kept promising, kept pursuing, kept chasing. He longs to dwell with his people, yesterday and today.

So he chases and goes to them, until silence. Four hundred years to be exact. But the promise still loomed that he would come.

And then Jesus shows up. God the walking temple. God in

flesh. The dwelling place of God is now walking among us. But many of the Jews missed him. They wanted power more than they wanted love and justice and mercy.

In fact, they go so far as to kill him. They put God on the cross. *We* put God on the cross.

You'd think God would have reached his tolerance limit and gotten rid of us all. Can you see all the pain and grief from God's point of view? Just think of a friend or sibling who's making poor decisions and choices, and how it literally hurts you. Now multiply that by billions, over thousands of years, and that's the pain we've caused God. He could have stayed high and lofty, but he knew love isn't possible without vulnerability.

So instead of blowing us off the planet after hundreds of years of rebellion, he resurrects from the grave and then sends his very Spirit to dwell in us! It doesn't get much more vulnerable than that. We can grieve the very Spirit of God because we are now his dwelling place, his temple.

God is forever taking one more step toward us, and every time he reveals himself, it's in a less guarded way. He wants to make himself known, and to do that he makes himself vulnerable.

The other gods seem high, mighty, and untouchable; they leave us to move first, to initiate, to appease them.

But this God, Jesus, says, "No. I'll go first. I'll lean in. I'll risk being hurt. I'll come down to you."

And he relentlessly pursues and chases. He shows that sooner or later, love will woo a human heart. Might we lean back in to him?

God in the temple, God in Jesus, and now God in us. And

the Scriptures keep going all the way to Revelation 21 where it says we don't need a temple because God is our very dwelling place.

If you want a strange verse about what will happen at the end of time, read Isaiah 11:9: "For the earth shall be full of the knowledge of the Lord, as the waters cover the sea."

The word *knowledge* used there is דֵּעָה in the original Hebrew, which can mean "intimate." It's not knowledge of mathematics or science; it's knowledge of intimacy. If you're married, you *know* your spouse.

This is also the verse that says at the end of time, when everything is fully restored, God's weight, glory, and knowledge will cover the earth the same way the water covers the sea.

The verse sounds cute and poetic at first, but if you think about it, it sounds strange.

How does water cover the sea? We lived on a little lake near the mountains in Washington, and it's man-made, so they drain it every winter. When I looked outside while writing this, it was practically empty and all that was left was a huge dirt-laced cavern with a bunch of stumps.

When they took the water out of the lake, they took the lake too. Water doesn't just *cover* sea; water *is* the sea. They are so interwoven that they are basically the same because sea is a type of water.

What God is saying is that when he finally gets his goal and is fully dwelling with his people, in full intimacy, and sin, death, and all evil is gone, his glory and beauty will be so deeply covering the earth and our lives that they won't be ever be able to be separated again. Similar to the water and the sea, his glory and the earth will be married fully as one never to be separated again.

Is that the trajectory your life is on?

The cool part about the Bible is we can read the ending. And every time I do, I have to ask myself, is my life going that direction? Toward closer intimacy with God? Toward beauty? Toward him dwelling with me? Am I allowing him to take up residence in my life in all things? He's coming down and being vulnerable, am I reciprocating and dancing back with him in the music of eternity?

The incredible thing about this is once you step into it, it never ends. Once we start following Jesus, every day our entire lives are about us getting closer and closer to our Creator. This isn't something you achieve or reach the finish line on.

Every day is a battle, and some days are better than others, but it's about resolving to put our moment-by-moment lives on that path. What can you do to put yourself on the right path? What little things can you do today to put you on the right trajectory? After all, you already know the ending.

CHAPTER THREE

PEOPLE ARE NOT WHO YOU THINK

THEY'RE NEIGHBORS TO LOVE, NOT COMMODITIES TO USE

THERE'S SOMETHING ABOUT SHAME THAT MAKES ME WANT TO HIDE.

When I was a freshman in college, my girlfriend came to visit me for a weekend. Since I was at a Christian college and girls couldn't stay in the dorms, we got a hotel room.

A boyfriend and girlfriend staying in a hotel room for the weekend doesn't usually lead to playing Scrabble into the wee hours of the morning. We were sleeping together at this point in our relationship. Since we would've said we were Christians, I was used to the usual cycle of lust, then shame, and then remorse every time we gave in.

But this time was different. Much stronger. Much sharper. The morning after, we realized we hadn't used protection and didn't even entertain the thought of what that might have meant until later. What if she got pregnant? What if we had just conceived a baby? What would we do?

And that's when one word pierced my mind sharper than a dagger: *abortion*.

It was the first time I ever entertained the thought. Up until that point I was always the guy who would argue with anyone who said they were pro-choice.

Don't they know it's a life? Don't they know it's not their life to take? Don't they know they shouldn't make bad decisions if they don't want to get pregnant?

I still believed those first two, but the last one was flipped because now it was *my life.* We couldn't have a baby because we were both in college and pursuing different careers. We couldn't have a baby because we had an extremely unhealthy and schizophrenic relationship (love one minute, hate the other). Neither of us wanted to be with the other forever, and a baby would have sealed that relationship. We couldn't have a baby because I was seen as a Christian, a good kid, and this would have ruined all that.

What if people found out? What would they think?

So that morning we drove to the grocery store, and she went in and got the emergency morning-after pill from the pharmacy department. And then we waited.

The next couple of days and weeks were some of the hardest I have ever gone through. I literally barely got through a day, since my mind was so incredibly focused on that one question, *what if?*

She didn't end up being pregnant, but I'll never forget that moment. The shame ran so deep, and so sharp, I can almost feel it seven years later. Not only did we feel shame as Christians having sex before marriage, but the hypocrisy of being pro-life in public but considering abortion in private compounded the feeling.

Shame has a slimy feeling, like it's starting to cover you, and you can't help it. Then the voices of condemnation and rejection start repeating in your head what you already think to be true. *Gross. Dirty. Not good enough.*

And when that feeling comes, we have the urge to hide. *Cover up. Lie. Shut down. Numb the pain.*

That wasn't the only time I've felt covered in shame and done everything in my power to hide. I remember feeling the same way when I got arrested at age fifteen for shoplifting. I remember feeling the same way when my sister or my mom found porn on the family computer—multiple times. I remember feeling the same way when I got caught plagiarizing in college, got an F in that class, and almost didn't graduate. Something in me crawled deeper into a hole. I felt naked, exposed, shamed, guilty, hurt, rejected.

Shame cuts us off from intimacy, vulnerability, and transparency. When humans' imperfections are exposed, our natural inclination isn't to step into the spotlight but to run away from it and hide. We cover ourselves and put on a mask.

But what's funny is, our first parents taught us about hiding.

Rewind back to the garden of Eden. God created this beautiful and amazing world and put image-bearing humans (Adam and Eve) there to care for it, create within it, and reflect him to it. He gives them one law: don't eat fruit from the Tree of Knowledge of Good and Evil.

As its name suggests, when the couple eats of that tree, they will *know* the difference between good and evil. This implies that before they eat it, they *don't* know good from evil. So as humans in the world tasked with a job, how are they to know? The only possible explanation is total dependency on God their creator.

The only way for them to avoid an evil they wouldn't recognize is to be leaning on God so completely that he tells them. So eating the tree is actually saying *no* to dependency on and intimacy with God.

We don't need you; we don't want you; we can do this on our own.

In the West, this doesn't sound very offensive; our entire culture is built on autonomy and a pull-yourself-by-your-bootstraps mentality. But ultimately we have to admit there's something in us that tells us we were created to do this life thing alone, but such independence leads to exhaustion.

But in the garden, that command not to eat from the tree wasn't some arbitrary rule. I always thought it was the weirdest command, as if God were tempting us to sin. Like, God, if you didn't want us to eat from the tree, then why put it there?

But the tree wasn't a temptation to sin; it was an invitation to intimacy. It was God giving humans the choice to live with him or without him. We can lean into him for what's right and wrong, since we don't truthfully know, or we can "eat the fruit" and have our own standards, ways, and paths. One choice leads to life, and the other leads to destruction.

And so in Genesis 3:5, Eve and Adam believe the words of a serpent, "You will not surely die. For God knows that when you eat of it your eyes will be opened, and you will be like God, knowing good and evil," and grab for the throne. Instantly they knew good and evil. Something cracks. Something breaks. The fruit promised something it couldn't deliver and the mirage falls away. The text says, "Then the eyes of both were opened, and they knew that they were naked." Exposed. Uncovered. Shamed. Guilty. Out in the open.

It goes on to say, "And they sewed fig leaves together and made themselves loincloths. And they heard the sound of the LORD God walking in the garden in the cool of the day, and the man and his wife hid themselves from the presence of the LORD God among the trees of the garden."[1] So the primal sin, the sin behind every sin, is saying, "I want to be like God. I want to know what's good and evil. I want to be fully autonomous. I want to sit on his throne."

Sin is less defined as smoking weed and stealing money from your boss and more defined simply as, *I know.* And whenever we say we know what's right and wrong, we become our own judge and God, and that can play out in all sorts of behavior that isn't the best for ourselves or human flourishing. Now, let me clarify that the issue isn't knowing right and wrong at all. The issue is *where* we find out right and wrong. Do we lean on God for what's right and wrong, or do we lean on ourselves? One creates life, one creates death.

But here's where I think the best part comes: That beginning part of the story shows the primal sin, but what's the primal response of God? We have the first thing the humans did, and then what's the first thing God did?

What's God's first reaction after the humans throw a wrench into the entire system of creation? They did *exactly* what God told them not to do, and so God had the right to punish, to condemn, or to take man off the earth.

But it says God walks around the garden and asks two questions: "Where are you?" And then, when Adam responds that he hid because he felt naked and ashamed, God then asks his second question: "Who told you that you were naked?"[2]

God is *God*, so I don't think he was playing a game of hide-and-seek with the first humans or looking for precise GPS coordinates.

"Adam, what bush are you behind, bro? I can't find you." No, the question was a rhetorical one. It was a plea and beckoning with ache in his heart. I can just imagine the sharp pain God must have felt in that betrayal moment. The beautiful world God had made, and the relationship with the humans had been perfect, yet both were thrown out of whack in one quick moment.

God could have gotten angry. He could have left them to be in their own curse, but he does something fascinating. He goes looking for them.

Adam, where are you?

My son, my daughter, where have you gone?

You don't need to hide from me.

God's voice is always calling us *out* of hiding—that's how you know it's God's voice. If you're in a season struggling to identify God's voice, maybe ask which voice is calling you out of hiding and into intimacy.

It's only when we stop hiding that we can start healing. Every time I've experienced deep joy in my life, it was because I came out of hiding, asked for help, and admitted I couldn't keep up the act anymore.

But it goes on. God finds Adam who, probably with his face down, laments that he was afraid because he was naked.

God asks another explosive question: "Who told you that you were naked?"[3]

Who told you that you weren't good enough?

Who told you I didn't love you?

Who told you that you were a failure?

Because I sure didn't.

And God's questions haven't stopped since this very beginning. Throughout history up to this very moment, those questions echo throughout schools, offices, baseball fields, and modeling agencies. Why are you hiding?

I've heard his voice in moments when I've desperately needed it. To all those stories in the beginning of this chapter, to failure on the baseball field, to times I've messed up and let a friend down, God whispers, "You're good enough for me. You are loved. You are mine."

His voice always calls us *out* of hiding and *into* intimacy because that is God's goal. He makes it clear from Genesis to Revelation that he wants to *dwell* with his people. He desires intimacy not hiding, transparency not masks. To know God and be known by God is the dance of eternity.

But the Scripture narrative shows us throwing wrenches into his plan. It's us continuing to eat fruit of the Tree of Knowledge of Good and Evil while God relentlessly pursues us. God's goal is to dwell with his people, but it's a two-way street. For that to happen, we have to come out of hiding and take off the masks. We have to be vulnerable. We have to have our ears tuned to the heartbeat of God.

And rather than forcing us into submission, God takes the long way and woos us back to him. He puts us on a trajectory that gets deeper and deeper into intimacy.

THE NARRATIVE OF SCRIPTURE

When you listen to the heart of God and hear him calling us back to the garden and to his heart, it's not just a one-time thing. The entire book of Genesis is about God continually asking Adam, "Where are you?"

The problem, though, is while Genesis is a beautifully crafted book, it is commonly misunderstood. As I mentioned in chapter 2, it's separated into two parts: the first twelve chapters and the last thirty-eight. The turning point in the narrative is the story of Abraham. Even the way the story is told takes a drastic change at Abraham.

Before we meet him, Genesis is full of event-driven narratives such as the division of Babel and the Flood, but the story of Abram-turned-Abraham extends for thirteen chapters! Thousands of years of history had less narrative attention paid to them than this one man, Abraham. I think that means it's pretty important. After Abraham the narratives are no longer event-driven but personality-driven. Abraham, Isaac, Jacob, and Joseph dominate the text.

So when we zoom out and view the whole picture of Genesis, we see that God has always wanted to be with the humans. Humans rebel and are banished. Humans then run and hide *east* of Eden. The theme of going east continues, mainly whenever something bad happens. It's as if running east is a picture of going away from of the garden, *away* from God, and away from intimacy.

We start to see it everywhere. When Cain kills his brother,

he is banished *east* into the land of Nod. Right before the tower of Babel was built, the people moved "eastward." When Abraham and his nephew Lot have an argument and split ways, Lot goes east toward Sodom and Gomorrah.

To go east is to go away from God, to go farther from the garden and his presence (which is why Steinbeck's famous book is called *East of Eden*). So throughout the first 12 chapters, everyone keeps going east. Things keep getting worse.

But then Abraham shows up. A man of faith, dependency, and vulnerability, Abraham is called to an unknown place and trusts God to get him there safely. And what direction does he travel? West.

Back toward the garden. Back toward the presence of God.[4]

Abraham then leads down the road to Isaac, Jacob, Joseph, and finally to Moses and the family of Israel. That's where I think a lot of us start to skip sections of the Bible. The narratives aren't hard to follow, and we learned a lot about them in Sunday school. We know the famous characters, and we can still remember the biblical artwork. But once the Bible starts getting into the laws of Exodus, Leviticus, and Deuteronomy, a lot of us are either bored or quite confused.

The name for that section of Scripture is called Law. Or the Torah, which can also be translated as "instruction." A lot of Christians, myself included, fumble with the Law. We settle for a false dichotomy that says law is bad but grace is good, or the Old Testament isn't relevant, let's just settle for Jesus (if you don't think we do this, next time you're in a hotel, check out the nightstand drawer. Good bet that if there's a Bible in there, it's a pocket

New Testament only). And if we do read the Old Testament, it's usually only Genesis, Psalms, and Proverbs.

God wouldn't give us something that was irrelevant. He's a good and gracious Father. He'd never give us something that wasn't for our joy. For our good. And yes it's tedious and extremely detailed, but that's because Israel had just been called out of four hundred years of slavery and had never been a nation with her own government, economy, and judicial system. They didn't have a codified religion either.

So God gave them 613 laws. It's like America's Constitution, the Apostles' Creed, and Luther's nintey-five theses rolled into one. Those documents, too, are tedious and detailed (and still get amended and reinterpreted regularly), but it was America's way of defining their identity.

Israel loved the Law; they wrote songs about it. David even remarks that the Torah is like honey on his lips:

> The rules of the LORD are true,
>   and righteous altogether.
> More to be desired are they than gold,
>   even much fine gold;
> sweeter also than honey
>   and drippings of the honeycomb.[5]

The law was their manifesto. A new way to live. A declaration of complete resistance to the way the cultures around them were living. It set them apart as people of God.

Others worshiped multiple gods; the Law declared there is but one God over all.

Others used, abused, and exploited one another; the Law said to love your neighbor as yourself.

Others said never stop working; the Law commanded Israel to rest, enjoy food and family.

Others said watch out for yourself; the Law says give a chunk of your crops to the poor.

The Law outlined a new way to live that instructed God's people to be the bearers of his world-rescue operation.

But there was one problem: Israel was not only part of the solution, but they quickly came to realize they were part of the problem too. They missed the point. They used the Torah to hide rather than obey the heart of it, which was to come out of hiding.

The Law was meant to bring the family of Israel into deeper intimacy, deeper fellowship with God. An entire book of the Torah, Leviticus, is devoted to proper worship of God, first in the tabernacle and then in the temple. God wanted to dwell with his people. He wanted to be on the ground with them. But for true intimacy to happen, it's a dance for two.

One of the tenants of the Law was obedience. Torah obedience is best summarized as "*if* you do this, *then* this blessing will come." And the opposite of Torah obedience was "if you fail to do this, then a curse will come." If you obey, you get blessed. If you don't obey, you get punished.

Now a lot of us cringe when we hear that. That surely can't be the character of God. Is that grace? Is that mercy?

Actually it is, and parents do the same thing. But that type of obedience is not meant to last forever. It's a tool to bring us into *deeper* intimacy. For example, when I was little, my mom would sometimes motivate me with candy so I'd do something or learn a habit—whether it was potty training when I was really young, or cleaning my room when I was a little bit older. "If you clean your room, you'll get a Snickers."

Now that sounds pretty normal, doesn't it? And honestly, bribery is an effective teaching tool, right?

But here's the problem: that type of motivation shouldn't last forever. It is good for a season, but if a Snickers bar truly does its job, then you soon won't need it anymore.

Let's fast-forward from childhood to college graduation. I haven't been home for the six months since Christmas break, and I'm excited to see my family. How weird would it be if I pull up and walk in the door, only to see my mom bend over, put her hands on her knees, and in a little kid voice say, "Little Jeffy, if you go clean your room, I'll give you a Snickers."

Talk about awkward. And just flat-out wrong.

A college graduate shouldn't use the bathroom, clean his room, do the dishes, and help his mom because he wants Snickers. My mom doesn't want to be the Snickers Provider forever—she wants to be *Mom*. Her Snickers put me on the journey of deeper knowledge and understanding. It formed and shaped and molded me. I now do those things because I love her and because those chores benefit me.

It's the same with God. The Law was meant to push the Israelites toward deeper intimacy with God. But Israel seems to keep going in circles, making the same mistakes and for long seasons abandoning God, before returning to him and restarting the cycle.

For example, in Psalm 51:16, David says, "You will not delight in sacrifice, or I would give it; you will not be pleased with a burnt offering." He got the fact God was after something *deeper*. The sacrificial system was an arrow pointing forward. Pointing deeper. Pointing to something more. He prefers his children not sin in the first place, and simply walk with him. Be with him. Know him.

The prophets understand this. Take Micah, for example. In chapter 6 he is reciting to the Israelites in Jerusalem the transcript of a trial. God is prosecuting his people for straying from him. Israel knows that no quantity of sacrifices will appease God, but Micah tells them what will: "What does the LORD require of you / but to do justice, and to love kindness, / and to walk humbly with your God?"[6]

He's drawing Torah obedience out to its logical conclusion: all God requires is that we "walk humbly" with him.

That's intimacy. That there would be a closeness. A nearness. A relationship. God was taking them somewhere. The Scriptures have a trajectory. Yes, there are cycles of disobedience and obedience, but each story moves the narrative forward.

This is why the Bible doesn't end how it starts. It starts in a garden but ends in a city. It starts with Law, but ends with intimacy. It starts with God in a tent, but ends with God in us.

CHECK OUT THAT VIEW

Right outside our backyard in Washington, Alyssa and I had this incredible view of Mount Rainier. We've hiked around the base of the mountain a few times, and it has one of the most breathtaking views I've ever seen.

Imagine we went hiking there but had never actually seen the mountain before. We had only heard about it from other folks, each one giving a little different description.

About a mile into the park we come to this big sign. It says Mount Rainier and it has a point on it. In our naiveté we think we've arrived. We say, this is it! We get out our phones and take selfies with the sign. We post them to let people know we saw Mount Rainier.

How weird would that be? We didn't actually reach Mount Rainier; the arrow was pointing us toward the right path.

What's fascinating is that's not too farfetched from what it's like with Jesus and us. The Old Testament is a sign pointing to the true reality.

Temple, sacrifice, Sabbath, and bread: they are pointing to something. They are pointing to the fulfillment of the promise to Abraham, but because God's children choose to worship signs instead of "walking humbly" with God, the first-century Jews missed Jesus, and we keep missing God.

Signs are needed on the journey. But once we reach our destination, it'd be absurd to continually return to the signs. And what's also interesting is signs don't give life. Just like with Mount Rainier, only the view of the mountain can amaze us and give us life.

It's at that moment of missing the signs so badly, that the very creation God made to reflect and show his beauty killed him. Isn't that absurd? No other god was ever that vulnerable.

I struggle with a meek, mild, victory-through-sacrificial-love type of God. I'm too used to power being shown through force. We learn from childhood that true power shows no pain.

But this God stoops low. Comes close. Reaches out and touches us. This God is humble. Hungry. Sad. He made himself vulnerable to the very creation he had made!

The question is, why? Because *intimacy is his goal*. And you only get intimacy by coming close and risking hurt, pain, and rejection.

C. S. Lewis famously wrote,

> To love at all is to be vulnerable. Love anything, and your heart will certainly be wrung and possibly be broken. If you want to make sure of keeping it intact, you must give your heart to no one, not even to an animal. Wrap it carefully round with hobbies and little luxuries; avoid all entanglements; lock it up safe in the casket or coffin of your selfishness. But in that casket—safe, dark, motionless, airless—it will change. It will not be broken; it will become unbreakable, impenetrable, irredeemable.[7]

Throughout the Scriptures you see God, risking himself to get his goal. From the call and ache of the garden all the way to Jesus' crucifixion.

When God sees that Cain murdered his brother, he asks, "What have you done?"

In Egypt, he considers a crime against his Hebrew people a crime against him. When Israel is disobedient to the point of destruction, to the cries of the prophets, God wonders when his children will get he just wants them, not their halfhearted sacrifice. Their full selves. Their hearts. Them without the masks.

And Jesus echoes this ache of God by saying how he longed to gather his people as a hen gathers her children, but the people were not willing. Even so it says he weeps over the city since they do not know the things that make for peace.

It's as if God was longing for *echad*, but his children weren't ready.

Echad is first mentioned in the garden. It says a man and a woman, when they join together, become *echad,* or *"one."* But that word *echad* is more explosive with meaning than just one flesh. It can literally mean to fuse together at the deepest part of our beings. Two becoming one, completely glued together, completely meshing.

I still remember one of the hardest conversations I have had with Alyssa. We were just starting to date again, and were sitting in the car after a wonderful date night. We knew marriage was a possibility on the horizon, and I felt like I finally had to share things in my past that would affect her if we got married.

I was incredibly nervous, as well as terrified of rejection or hurt, but I realized that if intimacy were to grow, I had to get vulnerable. For marriage to be what it truly is—two people becoming one in mind, body, soul, and spirit—I had to be honest.

I remember sharing with her many things, but specifically some details of my sexual past. My teenage years were littered with me almost worshiping sexual fulfillment in pornography, partying, and girls. And I say worship, because that was where I got my worth, value, and purpose as well as what I most lived for (which is what the definition of worship is).

I had to apologize and ask forgiveness from Alyssa for things I had done before I even knew her because of *echad*—one form of complete and utter intimacy. Because of that beauty, mystery, and power, God created it to function best in a man and a woman coming together for life and constantly *echading* or fusing together.

I needed forgiveness because I had betrayed *echad*. I had betrayed oneness. I had betrayed intimacy. And if I wasn't honest about it, it'd be a little part of my life or heart that Alyssa didn't know—thus blocking *echad*.

But something really peculiar happened in that moment. With the grace and forgiveness of Jesus, Alyssa forgave me. She heard all that I was and am, and still wanted to walk this journey with me. I still remember the tenderness in her voice as she spoke truth and forgiveness over me.

In that moment I was exposed and *known,* and yet because of Alyssa's grace, I was at the same time *loved.* And that is where intimacy is found—to be fully loved and to be fully known.

To be fully loved, but not fully known will always allow us to buy the lie that "if they only knew the real me, they wouldn't want me anymore." And to be fully known but not fully loved feels sharp, painful, at a level of rejection that hurts so bad.

But to be fully known and at the same time fully loved, now that is intimacy.

I don't want to give the wrong impression. Intimacy is certainly romantic in some aspects, but at its deepest level, it's much more than that. It can be experienced with friends and family, not just spouses and loved ones.

SCARED OF TRULY SEEING EACH OTHER

I absolutely love New York City. Maybe it's because my brain is going a million miles an hour and Manhattan is one of the only places where that speed feels at home, or maybe it's because I'm a huge New York Yankees fan (I know, I know—the team everyone hates).

The subway, however, is a very weird space. We are so close to other people on the subway. When I was riding it the other day, I took a second to look up from my phone and noticed just about everyone—and I mean literally almost every single person on the subway—was either looking down at their phone or glazed over looking straight ahead with their headphones on listening to music. I couldn't hear even one conversation between strangers, even though there were dozens of us in that one car.

Everyone was sharing this moment in the same confined space, yet everyone was in his or her own world.

We were together, but we were alone.

A subway car is designed for contact. The seats along the windows and the bars you grab onto if standing are all laid out so that it is extremely difficult not to be looking at someone else or even be right up against someone else.

It's intimate. But we are scared of that intimacy and retreat into our own worlds. Everyone is there, but no one is present.

Many in my generation get almost physically sick or anxious

when they are thrown into a situation like that and have no ability to pull out their phones. It's what we do to look busy, to retreat, to avoid eye contact, to avoid human interaction and intimacy (the catch-all term we use for this scenario is *awkward*—and heaven forbid we have to do anything that might take a slight relational risk and be awkward). With our phones, we can control the world we are living in. With our phones, we can crop and edit ourselves. With our phones, we can be the center of a social orbit. With our phones we can be *important*.

Have our phones—which Alexander Graham Bell developed to improve connectivity of relationships—delivered on their promise? What about "social" media? Texting? The Internet in general? They promised to make us feel more connected, yet we feel lonelier.

They promised to help us keep in touch, yet we keep lowering the bar of what that means. Scanning someone's Facebook profile is now seen as keeping in touch, and jumping on a phone call with another person is seen as too intrusive or intimate.

I cannot remember a time *without* the Internet and connectivity. I started texting in middle school, and MySpace became really popular at the beginning of high school. Technology is truly changing the way we think, interact, and love.

For example, I've been on too many phone calls when I put the phone on speaker so that I could use Twitter, check e-mails, and "get stuff done." Connectivity is making us more efficient but less connected. Relationships are not efficient; they are messy, time-consuming, and unpredictable.

With this connectivity, and our complete inability to sustain

relationships and intimacy, we are all love sick, intimacy defi-
cient, and completely relationally bankrupt; but no one thinks
so because we all are! It's only when someone is "healthy" that
people might start to realize that being sick is not normal.

One common side effect of emotional bankruptcy, too, is since
you don't have that anchor and peace, you fight to get it from anything or anyone else. You quickly begin to see people only in terms
of what you can get out of them, rather than what you can give to
them or do with them.

I think of Israel and Egypt. Pharaoh was a hard dictator who
judged people's worth and value based on their labor output. They
had to produce a certain number of bricks or a certain weight of
grain, or else they'd be whipped, maybe even killed. Their worth
was tied to how many bricks they could make.

That is turning divine-image-bearing humans into commodities.

What other areas do we do that in our lives? In the West,
commodification is the very air we breathe. We extort, stretch,
and abuse developing countries for their resources, and we give
nothing but a few bucks in exchange. It's all about being the most
efficient for the least amount of dollars. Everything has to have a
return on its investment. It's all about the bottom line. And that
way of living has bled into our relationships.

But that's true of products, not humans. The minute we make
an image-bearer of God into a product that can be exploited,
exchanged, or used for any type of gain, that is a sin.

This is why the Torah was so scandalous. When God calls
the Israelites out of Egypt, he turns their perceived identity as

commodities (you are only as good as what you do) to their true garden-given identity as image-bearers (you are good because you just *are*). God gave Israel a lot of the laws in the wilderness to turn their worldview upside down and say no. People are neighbors to be loved, not commodities to be used. Even the Sabbath is a sign of that.

In Walter Brueggemann's book *Sabbath as Resistance*, he talks about the Sabbath as a day when Israel resisted the spirit of Egypt. A day to put the flag in the ground and say we don't need to spin our wheels every second of every day. A day to rest and recognize neighbors. To love. To serve. To refuse to be sucked into commodification.

The lack of a Sabbath impedes our ability to have truly meaningful human relationships.[8] Our constant connectivity does the same, or it's at least numbing us to just how weighty and amazing human interaction truly is. Our eyes are blind to the glory of human existence.

Take the fascinating and extremely strange case of the North Pond Hermit. People in central Maine had been reporting strange accounts of missing household items since 1986. For almost thirty years, the entire community could point to various times they'd come home from work or a vacation, or wake up in the morning to realize something was missing. Because the items were so mundane—canned food, propane tanks, screwdrivers, tarps, etc.—some didn't even realize the things were missing for days, if not weeks.

When word got out, the North Pond Hermit became a legend. Was it one person? Why were all the items daily things? Why was jewelry never taken? Were people making this up?

The North Pond Hermit was Christopher Knight. One day in 1986 he decided he was going to live in the woods with zero human interaction. No one was quite sure why, but from that day forward, he didn't have any human interaction until the day of his arrest in 2013.[9] He had not made a phone call, spent any money, driven a car, written an e-mail, or seen the Internet. He lived in complete isolation.

It's a fascinating tale, and a story worth looking up, but one thing in particular in the interview he did after his arrest caught my eye: the interviewer made note of his awkward human interaction and inability to make connections. To explain this to the interviewer, he said, "I'm not used to seeing people's faces. There's too much information there. Aren't you aware of it? Too much, too fast."

When he was thrust back into human reality, it was too much. It was too weighty. It carried a glory to it that he couldn't even look at.

Even though Chris was broken because of his lack of human interaction, his reaction is instructive. They say you don't know the weight of something until it's gone. When human interaction was gone for so long and then reintroduced, he couldn't handle it. It was too much. Too heavy. Too much glory in another person. He wasn't used to it. There seemed to be a brokenness, an anguish—almost as if his humanness was diminishing and deteriorating in the woods.

Do you believe we are that weighty? That there's glory in our eyes? That each person's living, breathing body tells a story? That there is value in human interaction? There's intimacy in eye contact, in a hug, in being close, or even in a vulnerable conversation. By prioritizing the virtual world, we are losing that.

The first time God shows up in the Bible, it's plural. When we were created and molded by the very hands of our Creator, it says, "Let *us* make man in *our* image." That's strange because the Bible affirms over and over again that God is *one* (the very foundation of Jewish faith is the Shema—hear, O Israel, the Lord our God is *one*). Monotheism was actually, and is still very much so, a scandal.

However, there is a communal aspect to the nature of God: three persons, but one God. It's as if there is this dance going on between the Father and the Spirit and the Son for all eternity. The rhythm of service and self-giving love continues for all time, and out of that love and community was the creation of us.

And so the beautiful truth is that since we were created by a community, we were created for community. If we are made in God's image and God is a community, then that means we are rejecting our humanness when we live isolated and alone. That's fundamental to what it means to be human. That is intimacy.

CHAPTER FOUR

YOU AREN'T WHO YOU THINK

YOU'RE A PERSON FROM THE FUTURE

ONE OF MY FAVORITE MOVIES OF ALL TIME IS *BACK TO THE Future*. I got the special edition trilogy DVD set when it was released on Christmas back in high school, I dressed up as Marty McFly one year for Halloween, and I enjoy saying "Great Scott!" any chance I get.

When anyone is wearing a puffy vest in the winter, I immediately ask, "Ay kid, what's with the life preserver?" If they laugh and get the joke, I know we can be immediate friends. If they stare at me awkwardly, I know they are one of those poor souls who has never seen the movie.

One of the premises of the movie (and any time-travel movie for that matter) is when Marty goes back (or forward) in time, he stands out. He knows things, has seen things, and acts differently because he is from the future. In the first film, there are some scenes where he is thought of as weird for making really peculiar decisions because his peers don't understand where he's coming from.

I like to view Jesus followers in the same way.

If you jump back two thousand years to when Jesus was walking the earth, a majority of the Jewish people believed in the resurrection. They believed at the end of time, when God set the world right, the righteous would be resurrected and vindicated. The twist is that Jesus did that in the *middle* of history, not at the end. God did for Jesus in the present what Jewish people thought he'd do for all at the end.

In the resurrection, Jesus became a person of the future. He threw a lasso around God's future promise, and he ripped it into the here and now. He brought in a new world, a new way of living, a body that doesn't decay, one that is full of beauty and glory. And then he told his disciples to go and implement that. Go work it out. Bring that promised future into the present. And that's what Christianity is supposed to be.

Identity, or the idea of defining who we are, is primarily about living as if the future restoration has happened right now. It's imagining what will be true when heaven and earth are fully reunited and grabbing onto that now. Jesus has already resurrected, and that resurrection power is in every one of us who trust Jesus.

God calls us to live as our future selves right here in the present, and by his Spirit he gives us the power to do so. One of my favorite quotes is, "Easter was when Hope in person surprised the whole world by coming forward from the future into the present."[1] Some of you might think this is a little funky, but we see it all the time in our world. For example, we call someone president-elect after the election but before the inauguration. And he is allowed to put into practice in the now what will be true very soon in the future. He gets secret service detail and millions of funding from Congress before he takes office.

We also do it with kings. David, in the Old Testament, was anointed king long before he sat on the throne. But he was called, the minute he was anointed, to live as God's anointed one. He was called to pull the future into the present.

The question is, when does this start? Or to put it another way: where's the DeLorean?

For Jesus, it's his resurrection; but for us, we step into the future when we are baptized.

Baptism is a deeply mysterious and beautiful act in which we step into our future and declare we are identifying with Jesus in his death and resurrection. It's stepping into what God says is true about us.

Jesus' own baptism invoked deeply held stories of the exodus—the Israelites leaving Egypt, trusting God, and stepping through into their future, the promised land. The exodus story was arguably the most valued narrative of the entire Jewish faith. It is still celebrated as the time God rescued his people out of slavery. Israel itself went through its own sort of baptism coming through the Red Sea. When evil is left at the bottom of the water, they were referred to as God's firstborn or God's son. After Jesus' baptism, he heads into the wilderness as if he is Israel personified.

Of course Jesus didn't need to be baptized. He was clean. He was God. He was beautiful. But instead of standing back and pointing fingers, he jumps right in and identifies with his people. He steps into the waters as a way of saying, *I'm for you, and with you.*

And something crazy happens. He hears his Father's voice thunder down from heaven declaring, "You are my beloved Son;

with you I am well pleased."[2] The Father speaks Jesus' identity over him.

Remember, this is the *beginning* of Jesus' ministry. He had not done anything yet. No healings. No preaching. No cross. No resurrection. This voice came *first*.

A lot of times we do a bunch of stuff, and then hope the voice of approval and love will come after that. This basically describes my whole life. Trying to have a good year in baseball so my friends and coaches would tell me I'm awesome. Getting good grades so I could be affirmed. Being as religious as I could so others would think I was a good person.

We hope to hear we are children of God at the end of the road, but God thunders it in the beginning. We hop on the treadmill of life, hoping that when the timer runs out we will hear, "Well done, my child." When, in fact, God declares that over us *before* we get on the treadmill. It puts us on a new journey entirely.

Why do you do what you do? Why do you get up? Why do you work? Why do you play sports? Why do you try so hard in school? Is it because you're trying to get the Father to tell you he loves you, or are you giving life all your energy because you know he already *loves* you? When you live in the latter, you live more freely because you know failure isn't a deal breaker but an opportunity to learn and get back up again.

So back to Matthew's version of Jesus' baptism. God says Jesus is a son, a child. He is the *Beloved*. The word *beloved* implied a special affection or place in God's heart for Jesus. But the beautiful thing is when we trust in Jesus, we are wrapped up into him. So when we are baptized, we are stepping into the future. The future of belovedness that is true right now. You are God's beloved.

And God doesn't sprinkle his love; he drenches us in it. *My child, my child, my child. I am well pleased.*

Can you hear the Father's heart? Have you ever listened to his voice?

The crazy thing about water is it's able to get through every crack it encounters. It moves, changes shape, floods, and permeates every little crevice. That's how God loves. Where there is even the slightest hint of surrender and release, the slightest crack in our autonomy, God's healing love floods in.

I like how Jonathan Martin puts it in his book *Prototype*: the scandalous thing about Jesus and his baptism is that when God declared he was well pleased in him and that he was the beloved, Jesus *believed him.* He goes on to say, "And unlike every other person in human history . . . he never forgot."[3]

After we realize we are beloved, there sometimes comes a season when God wants to brand that into us. To let it sink in. Become real. If Jesus goes straight from baptism to ministry, preaching, healing, and the cross, God's voice might get drowned out. The noise is a powerful thing, and the noise of life can sometimes mute God's soft whisper of belovedness. But then something crazy happens. Jesus' hair is still wet as he starts walking toward the wilderness. He goes to the unknown. The place of chaos. The place where Israel wandered for years and years and years. Where they failed. Where people died.

A place of silence. That's where the future gets ripped into the present.

On our two-year anniversary, Alyssa gave me a sweet, thoughtful, long card of love and encouragement. One thing stood out to me though: she started speaking the future into the present me. She encouraged me by calling me steady, gracious, loving, and humble.

What's funny is that I don't think those are things I actually am. I try to be those things but fail frequently.

Anyone who's been encouraged by a loved one, a parent, or a close friend knows nothing fuses you more with strength, confidence, and peace than a person filling you up with encouragement like that.

When I read Alyssa's letter, I felt like a superhero. Now am I those things? Maybe feebly sometimes, but certainly not always. What's important, though, is that Alyssa believes I am and can be. And there's something deeply mysterious about it all, but when she says those things about me and constantly reminds me and encourages me, guess what? I start to become those things! It's as if she's speaking the future to me in the present.

If a loved one can speak such life, or such future, into us, then how much more power is there when the very Creator of the universe does it? He speaks over us, he delights in us, and when we are in Jesus, he tells us our futures are true right now in this very moment.

If you really believe that, and if you really listen to that, nothing can hurt or stop you. I know it might look good on paper right now, but do you really believe that? Have you heard that voice? Do you put your ear toward Jesus and listen?

GRABBING FOR WHAT WE ALREADY HAVE

I had never been one of those people who camps out for a special deal on Black Friday, but I was getting married a week later, and we were hoping to snag an awesome deal on a TV for our new place when the store opened at midnight. So we ended up going there late after dinner and joined the line bending around the block.

It turned out to be fun, standing in line with Alyssa and Susie, my mother-in-law-to-be. We chatted and enjoyed our time, and honestly we weren't going to be too upset if we didn't get the TV.

When midnight hit and they started letting people in, we realized we were probably the only ones with that take-it-or-leave-it attitude. People acted as if it were the apocalypse and they were diving for food rations or something. But no, this was for TVs, video games, toasters, and other stuff that would end up in garage sales in five to ten years or sooner.

It was chaos—people yelling, screaming, stampeding. They were jumping and running toward things they seemed to think they *had* to have. It was as if law and order had been suspended for those first few moments. I am not overstating it. People have been shot, pepper sprayed, and trampled to death over saving a few bucks on electronics.

This was an interesting picture of us and our identities sometimes. When we think we don't have something we need, we inevitably grab for it and hold on for dear life. When Adam and Eve decided to live without God, they *grabbed* the fruit.

That garden temptation sent them out of paradise and into

the desert. When the Israelites decided to worship Baal because Moses had been gone awhile, they grabbed for the security of another god. That fear kept them from entering the promised land and left them in the desert for a generation.

But Jesus went to the desert willingly, knowing he, too, would be tempted. First notice that all the temptations Satan offered asked Jesus to prove his (and God's) identity: "If you are the Son of God, command these stones to become loaves of bread. . . . If you are the Son of God, throw yourself down."[4]

Notice the showdown that happens. Satan says *if* you are the Son of God, then do these things. He was tempting Jesus to grab. But Jesus responds by saying *because* he's the Son of God, he doesn't need to do those things.

Satan tells Jesus to prove it.

Jesus tells him he doesn't need to because he already knows who he is.

You don't need to grab and claw for something you already have.

Satan tempts Jesus first with the physical desires. He's in the wilderness, probably on the cusp of passing out from hunger and dehydration, and Satan knows he has the power to turn rocks into bread. But Jesus doesn't because he knows his Father takes care of him. He doesn't need to grab for bread when his Father is the one who sustains.

Then Satan tempts him to test God. Think how many times we've put God to the test. But again, he knows he doesn't need to have God prove his love when the Father just called him beloved weeks before.

And the last temptation is a temptation of power. He can have everything if he just worships Satan instead. But Jesus knows he already has everything and God is the true King.

Only when we follow Jesus as the truly Human one, and the one who rightfully walks in his identity, can we, too, truly walk in who we are. Without following Jesus' footsteps, we are naturally prone to grab, to seize, and to clutch our identity in other things. We are all looking for security, not realizing we already have it in Jesus.

And when we realize we already have everything we need in Jesus, it's not about grabbing but abiding. Abiding. There's a reason we are called human beings not human doings. We abide and we be. We rest in what Jesus makes true of us the minute we begin to follow him.

WHAT VOICES DO YOU LISTEN TO?

The security that we have in Jesus doesn't do much for us unless we trust it and listen to it. Similar to a life vest, it only becomes helpful once we wear it.

One way to really rest in our identity is to make sure we are listening to the right voices. Identity is primarily a battle of voices. What do you listen to? Or who do you listen to?

In the first century, Jewish communities would hold a *kezazah* (literally, "to cut off") ceremony if someone from the village married a gentile women or sold family land to Gentiles. If the leaders of the community saw the offending man try to enter the village, they would grab him, bring him to the center of the village, and break a pot (usually filled with grain) at his feet. The pot was a sign of the community's relationship with the son. It was broken and could never be restored. He was cut off from the community, no longer welcome there.

This tradition seems to be lurking in the shadows of Luke 15 and the parable of the prodigal son.

The younger son asks for his inheritance, and then only a few verses later we are told he's already squandered everything and must hire himself out to feed pigs. It even says the pigs were eating better than he was! Not only do we sense the deep despair and low point, but the cultural shadow looming in this text is he lost his inheritance, and the place he lost it was with someone who owned pigs, namely a gentile.[5]

As he approaches his father's tent in disgrace, an incredibly scandalous thing happens: The father *ran* to his son. Running was a deeply shameful thing for Middle Eastern men to do. That was for children, not for a dignified and proper patriarch. But the father was willing to bear that shame because he wanted to be the first person to greet his son. The father would have known the kezazah ceremony was warranted, so he ran to make sure his was the first voice over his son. He spoke truth:

"You're loved."

"You're known."

"I don't see your mess; I just see you."

What's the first voice over you? It's the voice of a Father running to you with open arms. It's a Father declaring that you are his child. (Notice, in that story the Father immediately goes into declarations that explicitly meant sonship—the robe, the ring, and the party.) The son didn't have to do anything to earn passage back into the family. He was lavished with grace, love, and mercy. And the robe and the ring even meant he got more inheritance! All the Father had was now his again, simply because love made a way. God's voice creates inheritance, speaks love, and gifts mercy.

When voices come, which do you listen to? Shame? Guilt? Disgust?

Or do you listen to the first voice over you? It's called the *first voice* because it was there back in the garden before anything else started to compete with it. The voice that's been calling over you since the beginning. The voice that started in the garden and has echoed down to us now: "My son. My daughter. My child. My beloved."

I'm not telling you to trust the first voice that comes in your head. I'm saying that God's voice was before anyone else's voice, and that's the one we should be listening to. I know how hard it is to recognize God; I've almost trained myself to listen to the voices of shame and failure. I recognize the enemy's voice more than God's because for so long I listened to his instead of to Jesus.

When we are in the Scripture—the Gospels specifically—on a daily basis, then Jesus' voice is clearer. These ancient texts, narratives, and songs have a way of waking my heart to the Holy Spirit. How awesome is that?

The tough question is, do we even leave space in our hearts to hear that voice? When we are looking at our phones while in line at the store, when we are bored at home, when we are waiting for something to happen, then we might be listening to the voice of emotional bankruptcy. We are always listening to voices—on TV, on the Internet, from our friends. Do you know the difference?

God speaks in the quiet. The wilderness is a place of utter silence. Have you ever been in a room so silent it was deafening? As if you could audibly hear your own thoughts?

Silence is this eerie monster that a lot of us try to avoid. We run from silence because we are scared of its power. Silence can make us face our true selves. It's when we begin to ask the deep questions. That's probably why we check our phone right before bed and right when we get up—so that we don't have to sit in the uncomfortable silence. That gnawing feeling of inadequacy. The temptation to grab. That sense of not measuring up or being good enough. We can drown it out with technology and all sorts of noise, but in silence it seems to pummel us.

When we cut out silence, we cut out the margin for God to speak.

The prophet Elijah learned this lesson in 1 Kings 19. Right before this, Elijah, an incredible voice for God, has defeated an entire army of false prophets in an epic showdown where God literally rains down fire onto a drenched altar to show that he is the one true God. Elijah stands alone as the one who never waivers or loses hope that Yahweh is God when everyone else is worshiping the false god Baal.

In no fewer than just a couple of sentences Elijah is already on the run with his tail between his legs, distrusting God and being utterly afraid. The story first of all is a hilarious and huge encouragement to all of us who know we can change our trust of God that quickly. One minute we're on a mountaintop, and the next we're in a valley. We are all a mixture of glory and dust, faith and doubt.

But what happens next is quite peculiar. God comes and visits Elijah with an audible voice (there's a theme all throughout of God coming after us, as we've seen). But the writer of 1 Kings makes certain to show us what God was *not* speaking in.

It first says a great strong wind tore through the mountains and broke rocks into pieces, but "the Lord was not in the wind." Then it says an earthquake occurred, but the Lord was not in that. Then a fire, but the Lord was not in the fire. And Elijah hears a gentle sound; God blew like a soft wind and spoke in a low whisper.

When I think of *whisper*, I think of tenderness, gentleness, beauty. And that was God's voice. The hard part with whispers, though, is we have to be listening for them. They are just loud enough that only the people listening will hear and those who are distracted won't.

That's the importance of the wilderness. It's a place where we can hear the whisper. It's a place that isn't drowned out by the noises of our phones, computers, and twenty-four-hour news cycle. Wilderness is sometimes the only place we can hear the voice of God.

Jesus went into the wilderness to let his belovedness soak in. Do you do the same thing?

A lot of us curse the wilderness. *Something must be wrong*, we think. We must be sinning. But what if the wilderness is a gifted time to learn your belovedness?

There's a strange verse in the Old Testament by the prophet

Hosea in which God says to the Israelites, who were in a season of rebellion, that he is going to "lure them into the wilderness and speak tenderly to them"—which sounds crazy. The wilderness represented death, ache, pain, no food, and thirst. Yet God said He was going to lure them into the wilderness. There's this romance in that word *lure*; it's as if God is wooing them into the wilderness. He wanted to speak tenderly to them. God sees the wilderness as a special place between us and him. What if we stopped rejecting it?

WHO YOU KNOW IS BETTER THAN WHAT YOU DO

In elementary school I was quite the problem child. I was bored. And when a little boy is bored, he usually gets into trouble.

Routinely I'd do things such as turn off the lights in the bathroom when boys were in it, shoot spit wads at other kids, and other dumb stuff ten-year-olds do.

A lot of my mischief happened during recess. I'd throw something at a kid, kick a ball at them, or say something to egg them on. Now, I am not the tallest or biggest guy, and elementary school was no exception. I was arguably the smallest kid in every class until high school. So when I would do stuff like this, I knew I had to be able to outrun the kids because I sure couldn't outfight them if they came after me.

Eventually I learned I didn't have to run forever. I just had to run fast enough to my friend Big Mike. His name is pretty self-explanatory, and I'm sure my imagination is fooling me, but I remember a five o'clock shadow, flannels, and axes at age nine.

I was one of his closest friends, and the beauty of that is, if I did something stupid and a kid started to chase me on the playground, I just had to run to the safety of Big Mike's shadow. If I got there, the other kid would stop dead in his tracks and just give a look. I was safe, and they wouldn't touch me since I was next to Mike.

When those kids wanted to beat me up, they didn't stop because of anything I did. They stopped because of who I was with. They stopped because they weren't scared of me, but scared of him.

That's a little bit of what it means for Jesus' identity to be our identity. The phrase "in him" pops up in the New Testament more than one hundred times (which, by the way, if something is pushing triple digits, it's probably an important theme). What's true of Jesus is true of us, and when we trust him, he is our advocate. Anytime Satan whispers lies to you, you can just point to the person next to you. Jesus is blameless, which means we are too. He's righteous, which means we are too. He's got perfect access to the Father, which means we do too.

Too many times we try to defend ourselves when false voices start coming into our heads. But in defending ourselves we feel the ground slip beneath us. Instead we should run to the one who is our identity, Jesus himself. Demons aren't scared of us, but they are scared of him, and he's our advocate.

We are also children of the King, and that makes us dangerous. An attack on us is an attack on the royal family. You don't mess with the prince, because you're scared of the king.

Have you ever seen those movies that involve a king? There's usually at least one scene where they want to show the opulence of the throne room so the double doors whoosh open and with a super-wide-angle lens we start moving down the red carpet toward the throne. Most often, though, right next to the king we see his guards. Usually in some type of armor, with a dead serious look on their faces.

They look stiff, frozen, and cold. They are employees of the king, and they have a job to do. If they mess up, more likely than not they get fired. How weird would it look if the guards just started dancing around the throne room, running in circles, playing with their weapons, and jumping up and down with glee?

But that scene wouldn't seem out of place if they were children. There's this freedom afforded to children that they can have a playfulness about them. It would only go to show the tenderness of the king's heart if you entered the throne room to see kids running around the throne, jumping up and down, and having fun with daddy.

The kids have different privileges than the guards. But sadly, a lot of us pretend we are the guards. With God we are stiff, cold, serious, and afraid of getting fired. We are walking on eggshells. But a kid doesn't get fired. A kid can have that joy and freedom that only a kid can have.

Which picture more describes your relationship with God?

Are you terrified you are going to mess up all the time, or are you playfully running around God's throne knowing your dad is the King of the universe? God didn't come to make guards; he came to find his children. Jesus didn't hear "This is my employee" at his baptism; he heard "This is my beloved Son, with whom I am well pleased."[6]

When you look at your life, what do you see? Are you burned out? Are you tired? Exhausted?

There are voices creating that exhaustion. Voices creating that hurt. But there's another voice, a greater voice, a primal voice that is declaring over you right now that you are loved. You are known. You can run to the Father and know he will catch you.

CHAPTER FIVE

THE SABBATH'S NOT WHAT YOU THINK

YOU REST AS YOU PLAY

DEVOTIONAL AUTHOR LETTIE COWMAN WROTE ABOUT A TIME when she visited Africa. She was hoping to make the trip fairly quick, so she found particular guides she thought could help her make it as efficient as possible. During the first day of the trip, she was pleasantly surprised with how much progress they had made. On the morning of the second day, however, all the guides refused to move and stayed seated. Since she had hired and was paying these guides, she was frustrated and asked the leader why no one was continuing the trek—especially at the pace that was seen the day before. He responded by telling her they had traveled far too fast, and gone too far too quickly, and how they were "waiting for their souls to catch up to their bodies."[1]

When was the last time you rested and let your soul catch up? When I look back and try to answer it, I'm afraid my soul, my well-being, might not be just days, but years behind me.

The word *sabbath* literally means "to cease."

When's the last time you ceased? Unfortunately many of us can't answer that question because we don't know.

A lot of us would respond, "But there's too much to do! We don't have time to rest!"

Resting would sometimes seem ridiculous with how much we have on our plates. If we rest, we might get fired at our new job. Or, finals are next week, so how could we take a day off from studying? For me it hits home being a new parent. If you have a kid under the age of one, you know it's incredibly difficult to truly rest. But when I fight for that space for me, for Alyssa, and for our family, it is worth it. It's always worth it.

John Piper said, "One of the greatest uses of Twitter and Facebook will be to prove at the Last Day that prayerlessness was not from lack of time." We all have time. It comes down to how we spend it.

We all like to say we're busy, but are we really? Maybe busy on our phones for hours a day and in front of the TV or computer for another couple.

If someone approached you and offered the incredible gift of an extra day every week—meaning instead of seven days, every week is now eight days long—would you take it? What if the only caveat was you could only have the day if you didn't work. You had to play, enjoy family, eat a good meal, do something that fills and stirs your soul. Then would you take it?

We already have an extra day a week for that *exact* thing. God already built a day of rest into the rhythm of the universe. A way it works and moves, which if we step in line with fits best.[3]

Think about the beauty of dance. Ever since we've had Kinsley, we have mini–dance parties in our house from time to time. There's something about music and dancing that over-whelms Kinsley with joy. She can't help but start laughing and smiling. When she laughs, then we laugh, and we realize it's a fun and special moment for us as a family.

The funny thing about dancing, though, is you are not in control of the rhythm. You don't dictate the terms; the music does. If you're offbeat, it doesn't work. But the minute you step into the song, into the rhythm, you just know it feels right. Rhythm is a law, and everything works when we follow it.

It's the same with the Sabbath. There is a fabric, a beauty, and a dance of the universe, and we are dying because we aren't listening to the music. What if we tuned our ear to hear the music and rhythm of the cosmos? It just might change our lives.

When was the last time you asked someone how they were doing and they answered, "Great!" or, "I feel so peaceful and filled up right now"?

I'm guessing you can't remember. Instead people answer, "I'm just so busy right now!" or, "Work is really killing me. I feel like I have no time off." It's almost as if busyness is the new badge of honor. If you don't answer "busy" when someone asks you how you're doing, you immediately feel judged. You don't want people to think you're lazy or unimportant. It's a gross and twisted society when whoever works the most and whoever is most burned out is seen as successful.

We can say Jesus is our God, but it looks like work is our functional savior. If they added Performance and Work as an option under the Religious Views section of Facebook, maybe we'd be more honest.

We are afraid of rest. Afraid of silence. Afraid of idle time.

And I think there are two reasons for that: (1) we are terrified of silence, and (2) we are afraid of being unimportant. When we are resting or not doing any work, especially in the Western world, we feel as if we lose our identities. We no longer know who we are. That's why people are willing to sacrifice their whole lives on the altars of their jobs; at least then they think they look important.

There was an incredible study done by Timothy Wilson, a psychology professor at the University of Virginia, that shows just how addicted people are getting to being connected constantly. He noted that we are arguably the first generation with no idle time. Wilson conducted eleven different experiments with more than seven hundred people and discovered that a "majority of participants reported that they found it unpleasant to be alone in a room with their thoughts for just 6 to 15 minutes."[4]

People couldn't be alone with their thoughts for the same amount of time it usually takes to take a shower (maybe that's also why most creative ideas come in the shower, because it's the only truly idle time left).

Here's the frightening part of the study: There was an electric shock mechanism in the room that they could use to administer electric shocks to themselves if they desired. Previously the group had essentially said they would pay money to *avoid* being shocked.

After the idle time, though, "64 percent of men and 15 percent of women began self-administering electric shocks when left alone to think." Because we don't have the space to think and figure ourselves out regularly, we're scared of the difficult problems that remain unsolved. The study quoted examples such as "difficult relationships, personal and professional failures, money trouble, health concerns and so on." When we are finally alone with our thoughts, they scare us and force us to confront difficulties. We'd rather be online where things are already figured out. Or apparently administer electric shocks to ourselves.

Can that be any crazier? People would rather electrocute themselves than sit in silence.

Comedian Louis C. K. told Conan O'Brien about how silence makes us do incredibly foolish things:

> Sometimes when things clear away, you're not watching anything, you're in your car, and you start going, "Oh no, here it comes. That I'm alone." It starts to visit on you. Just this sadness. Life is tremendously sad, just by being in it . . . That's why we text and drive. I look around, pretty much 100 percent of the people driving are texting. And they're killing; everybody's murdering each other with their cars. But people are willing to risk taking a life and ruining their own because they don't want to be alone for a second because it's so hard.[5]

I'd be lying if I said I've never texted and driven for that same peculiar gnawing of quietness.

Also, in the spirit of self-disclosure, I've checked my phone, Twitter, and Facebook five times since starting this chapter.

The worst part is, technology is only priming us to go faster and faster and faster.

Remember fifteen to twenty years ago when dial-up 56k Internet started to be a thing? It sounded like a dial tone, then an incredible mash up of static and harsh sounds. It seemed like a miracle. We could get on the Internet, check anything we wanted, hear "you've got mail," and chat with others around the world. Remember when no one could be talking on the landline while on the Internet, and it wasn't a big deal?

If we were on a connection that slow today, we'd probably freak out and be immensely frustrated and throw something out the window. We are conditioned to want more, faster, better.

Scientific studies show that our need for speed is killing two huge parts of what it means to be human—creativity and empathy. Not giving ourselves time to rest impairs our ability to empathize. When we finally slow down, we start thinking of others. We aren't as self-absorbed, and we have time to give and be compassionate. Resting can create a better world when millions, if not billions, of followers of Jesus are setting aside a day to play, rest, and love.

Instead, our absolute addiction to noise and technology is fracturing and splintering us to death. Arguably the most notable and scholarly voice on how technology affects our rest, rhythm, and personality is MIT professor Sherry Turkle, who has dedicated her research to this very topic for the past thirty-plus years.

In a recent *New York Times* article, she discusses how our addiction to documenting every moment of our lives (such as taking pictures of our coffee and Bible and posting on Instagram, or posting a picture of what concert we are at on Facebook) is fundamentally changing us as humans.

As she puts it, "The selfie makes us accustomed to putting ourselves and those around us 'on pause' in order to document our lives. It is an extension of how we have learned to put our conversations 'on pause' when we send or receive a text, an image, an e-mail, a call. When you get accustomed to a life of stops and starts, you get less accustomed to reflecting on where you are and what you are thinking."[6]

We either pause moments or are present in the moments. We can't have both.

SPIRIT OF SABBATH

I love big cities, history, and culture; so naturally Jerusalem is one of my favorite cities in the world. (New York City might be a close second.) Even though I've only been there once, it was for a good chunk of time, and it wasn't the usual Western Christian trip. We saw the "Jesus sites," but that was only a day or two out of our journey.

We were staying with a mentor friend and family member whose family splits time between the states and Jerusalem. They have an apartment just a mile or so from the Old City, so we were in the middle of everything.

One of my favorite parts about being there was the celebration of Shabbat. On Friday night at dusk, a huge horn blows in the western part of the city that signals to everyone it is Shabbat. Within a few moments, instead of hustling and bustling, all you hear is silence. Besides the occasional car, practically no one is walking, driving, or outside at all, for that matter. It's kind of eerie.

For part of the city, though, it seems sometimes the law of the Sabbath is more revered than the Spirit of the Sabbath.

The Shuk, or the farmers market in the heart of the city, is absolute chaos Friday afternoon. Everyone is trying to get everything they need for three or four meals since everything will be closed Saturday. You can hear the anxiety and restlessness enter into the supposed rest. There are people yelling and hurrying everywhere. It seems many shoppers think their needs are more important than everyone else's, so you'd better get out of the way. Now of course this isn't everyone, and many people go about Sabbath preparation in a life-giving way. But for many it has become a burden. A chain.

I just can't believe this is God's intention for the Sabbath. Most are technically honoring the law, but their hearts aren't in it. It should create an atmosphere of beauty, and joy, and fullness. Working frantically to enter into rest is backward, to say the least.

The family we were staying with, however, had a beautiful rhythm, and the entire family seemed to partake in the preparations. They'd light a candle as a sign or put a stake in the ground of remembrance. That candle would burn the entire twenty-four hours. Then to begin Sabbath there would be a reminder that this day was about ceasing, about resting, about enjoying. The parents would pray and bless the five kids, and then we would all, usually emphatically led by the kids, bang on the table and clap our hands and sing a Shabbat song before dinner. Then we'd open a bottle of wine and have an amazing meal.

There was something sacred about it. Something mysterious. Something beautiful. No electronics. No looking down at our phones or scarfing down food so we could go play video games or watch TV.

Now that is a Sabbath. When I was at their table, I realized this was what life was about: Relationships. Food. Deep conversations. Intimacy.

We were there for a few Fridays, so we got to enter into their rhythms more than once. The next week was one of those rare moments (I can only recall a handful) when I felt the tangible presence of God and a weight of love and grace I had never before experienced.

It was about an hour before Shabbat dinner, and the family had decided to have a time of worship with another family who lived above them. We sang, we prayed, we celebrated, and we remembered what God has done for us.

At that time Alyssa was about four months pregnant with Kinsley, and because of her being pregnant and the fact we were their guests, they asked us to put our two chairs in the middle of the circle so they could encourage and pray for us. They surrounded us and laid their hands on us, which immediately added another level of intimacy and touch. I remember feeling so humbled in that moment.

They began thanking God for us, thanking God for this new life he was giving us, and thanking God for our future as a family. Even the kids prayed for us. To have eight different kids ranging from five years old to teenagers lay their hands on us and pray for us was humbling beyond belief.

In that moment I felt fully human. Fully loved. Fully known. Heaven had crashed into earth and set up an altar. Time seemed to pause, and love flooded in. The emotions still feel fresh just thinking about it right now.

That's a Sabbath I'll never forget.

Rabbi Abraham Heschel makes the point that what temple is to space, Sabbath is to time.[7] Meaning, a temple is a sacred space. A place where heaven and earth meet in a physical place.

Sabbath is when heaven and earth meet in time—in a moment. Especially in our Western work-addicted society, we need to set aside sacred time that resists the addiction to work, technology, and consumerism. Time isn't sacred to us. It's a commodity, and we all treat it as such. It almost shocks me to realize that for the larger part of history, they didn't have clocks and endlessly plan the day out to every minute—eat at this time, five work meetings during this time, take the kids to soccer practice at this time. We are slaves to time in Western society.

Honoring Sabbath is saying no; time is sacred. But what should this time be set aside for?

When we read the New Testament, we see the purpose, heart, and mission behind Sabbath changes as the Christian church matures. A lot of people think Sabbath is being quiet, praying all day, or just completely vegging out on the couch.

While that can be a part of Sabbath if done right, I'd argue that it can be anti-Sabbath. A quiet miserable day of beating yourself up over all your sins, isolating yourself (and alienating others) while you pray, or just killing time until Sunday is actually anti-Sabbath.

As a young family, Alyssa and I are right thick in the middle of learning how to Sabbath, how to set aside time to really care for our souls. We are always tweaking and discussing as a family, but a few things consistently put us in a Sabbath mood: (1) turning off our phones for a day, (2) doing something outside with nature, and (3) having an exceptionally good meal.

And those things came from us looking a little deeper into the trajectory of Scripture. When you look at the Bible as a whole, three principles pop up in relation to the Sabbath that help us honor it well by filling, remembering, and predicting.

The first purpose of the Sabbath can only be understood when we go back and listen to the garden echo. The Sabbath is a rhythm deeply woven into the cosmos. It's part of creation's DNA. God didn't rest because he needed rest; Genesis 2 tells us the rest was a celebration, an inauguration. A day of filling the earth with his presence.

So if God on the first Sabbath flooded the earth with his presence to both signify the completion of creation and have a day to especially fuse himself to that creation, then it only makes sense to celebrate it the same way.

What if one day a week we filled the earth with God's presence, being creative with our wallets, time, and energy? Sacred time to serve and love. I can't say Alyssa and I do this one well, but we're learning.

Maybe you invite your neighbor over for dinner on Sabbath. Maybe you see a widow down the street and ask if you can help around the house one day a week.

Maybe entering into rest means working on Sabbath. But if you've ever done something for others and remarked how it "filled you up" after the fact, you'll realize that's exactly in line with what Sabbath is supposed to be.

My favorite definition of the Sabbath is from Abraham

Heschel: "A reminder of every man's royalty; an abolition of the distinction of master and slave, rich and poor, success and failure. To celebrate the Sabbath is to experience one's ultimate independence of civilization and society, of achievement and anxiety. The Sabbath is an embodiment of the belief that all men are equal and that equality of men means the nobility of men. The greatest sin of man is to forget that he is a prince."[8]

Notice how all the things that the world usually says make us unequal are things that have to do with work—how much money we make, what kind of cars we drive, and what our jobs are. But on the Sabbath we are all equalized. Once a week we get to shatter the idea that we are on different levels. We are all human image-bearers of God, and everyone (while resting) is the same, we are reminded that is God's ultimate heart.

When we were prayed over and encouraged and loved, that was Sabbath. That was filling the moment with God's presence just as he did in the garden. It's ripping heaven down to earth and letting the moment be sacred. Sabbath is a day we can encourage others. Who could you text with a message of appreciation?

Are your days being filled, or are you always being drained? We need to set aside time for filling.

One really fascinating thing I don't hear many preachers talk about is that even though the Sabbath was the seventh day of creation, it was Adam and Eve's *first* day of life.

Put yourself in Adam's shoes. He wasn't there for the moon and the stars. The animals. The plants. He was the crowning act of creation. When God breathes life into his nostrils, he becomes a living being. Then God rests. From Adam's perspective, the first full day he saw as a human was a day of rest. The day of filling.

God did all the work, and Adam got to start with rest. Only after he'd been properly filled could he live up to his vocation as a garden-cultivating image-bearer. For God it was six days of work and then rest, but for Adam his first day was rest, and only then could he truly work. That sounds a lot like the cross, doesn't it? Jesus does all the work, and we are called to enter into that rest. Our first day, the first moment we open our eyes, is supposed to be a day and moment of rest.

Is the Sabbath seen as a beginning to the week or an end to the week? A lot of us, if we are working anxiously, can't wait to have a day off. That is fine, but I've noticed a different depth about my walk with Jesus every week when I set the precedent of observing the Spirit of Sabbath. Start with rest, then work. Don't work, then hope to get rest.

The Sabbath evolves after the exodus. After God takes the Israelites out of Egypt, he gives them the Torah. The Sabbath commandment is first found in Exodus 31, but it is revisited in Deuteronomy 5. There God explains that it's because they are to remember that God brought them out of their slavery in Egypt.

He tells them to take a day off every seven days because they are no longer slaves. They are free.

So the second purpose of Sabbath is that it reminds us that we are free.

If we aren't sabbathing, the question is, are we free? Or are we slaves to performance, to our phones, to being needed, to being in the know, to pleasure, to addiction?

A Sabbath is a day to celebrate and remember we are free people. We aren't under the empire anymore; we are under the kingdom. We aren't commodities; we are people. We aren't brick-makers; we are image-bearers. And when we remember, we free ourselves to have true community.

When we are commodities, other humans are competition.

When we rest, other humans are neighbors.

Growing up I always thought that if I wanted to be a Christian, I'd have to give up on fun. It was dismal, dark, and sacrificial. It is at times, but on the flip side it's also a faith of celebration. Christianity is one huge party. He's here! God is among us! Look what he's done! He's saved us! So let's celebrate. And sabbathing is doing exactly that. It is setting aside one day a week to party. To dance. To eat. To sing. And to love.

The Sabbath command is the fourth command. It looks back on the three about God and looks forward to the last six about how to treat people. It's the link between honoring God and loving people. And a true party does both of those things. It honors God, and it honors people.

Whenever Alyssa and I have a special dinner, we've started to do a prayer and a toast. A prayer to honor God, and a toast to look our guests and friends in the eyes and honor them. Sometimes it's nothing more than just saying we're thankful they are in our lives. But even a small dose of love can bring life in the same way the tiniest match can bring light in a dark room.

We've noticed that while it is always work to put together a gathering or a meal on the Sabbath, entertaining is one of the truly restful and life-giving ways we experience the Sabbath the most. This would have been unheard of before Jesus came, but when he came he began to question how rigidly and not exactly life-giving people were experiencing the Sabbath.

The Sabbath is the only commandment challenged by Jesus and eventually by Paul. All other commandments are still assumed to be in place, but the Sabbath commandment seemed to get tweaked or reshaped after Jesus. People were keeping it religiously, and in certain cases it sounded as if it was condemned.[9]

The people living in the first century had missed the point. They had made it an incredibly rigid day and bickered about what you could and couldn't do on the Sabbath. It became a day of technicality. The minute the fine details about what's right and what's wrong on the Sabbath creep up, you're far past what the heart of it is. They lived by the letter of the law, not the spirit of the Law.

We saw this attention to detail in Jerusalem when we were there in 2014. They have what they call Shabbat elevators, which stop on each floor, open the doors, and then continue that for the twenty-four hours. This is so an orthodox Jew can use the elevator without having to touch anything electric (such as buttons) and break Sabbath, because that would constitute work.

Jesus made it pretty clear, though, when he said the Sabbath was made for man, not the man for the Sabbath. We have a day that God made for us; don't turn it into a day of slavery.

The day is a gift. It's a filling. It's not a burden or a legality meant to be technically obeyed. It's a day when we jump into God's presence head first and don't worry every five seconds about whether or not we are breaking it.

As we discussed in chapter 2, the temple was a building, but Jesus turned tradition on its head and said the temple was only a shadow. He was the true temple. The temple was wherever Jesus went. The place where heaven and earth met now walked and moved and breathed. And when we become Jesus-followers that becomes true of us.

So it is with Sabbath. In the same way Jesus exploded the temple out of the four walls, so Jesus exploded Sabbath out of one day. The Sabbath was an arrow pointing to the full renewal of all things. When full rest, and filling, and grace would be brought forth. When we honor Sabbath, we are pointing to the future when that will be true forever. Every moment will be a Sabbath moment in the restoration of all things.

Simply put, Sabbath is a calling for delight.

If we know that at the full restoration of all things everything will be made new, there will be pleasures forever more, there will be a feast and table we sit at with Jesus, then Sabbath is making that true right now. Sabbath is ripping that future delight right here into this moment. That's why a great meal is such a beautiful act of Sabbath worship. It's pleasure. It's delight.

I love the idea that Sabbath is simply about play. True play. Remember when you were a little kid and you played? You'd go out into the neighborhood, think of incredibly creative games when all you had was a can or a stick, and come back right before it got dark? That childlike sense of play is an echo of eternity. When you're playing, you're right next to the heart of God. You're tasting the future, because ultimately that's what the new heavens and new earth will be like. There will be worship of Jesus, and in that worship will be true enjoyment forever knowing this is what we were created for, and that will be play.

In Matthew Jesus says to enter the kingdom we have to become like little children. And I'd say one of the biggest markers of children, that isn't always true of adults, is they know how to play. Don't lose that. It's a signpost to the great feast where we are guests of the King.

Do you treat the Sabbath as a day of delight or a day of boredom? What fills you up? What gives you delight? What makes you feel new?

Whatever your answer—if in line with the new heavens and earth ethic—then do that thing. Paint. Eat. Laugh. Hike.

That's Sabbath, and that's worship.

CHAPTER SIX

WORSHIP'S NOT WHAT YOU THINK

YOU BECOME WHAT YOU BEHOLD

WHEN I WAS IN HIGH SCHOOL, I PLAYED ON THE BASEBALL team. We were pretty good—picked to win the state title and even ranked nationally. During spring break, we had a few games but no classes; so we'd get to the field early, warm up, and have time for a few competitive games.

One of the games was a scrimmage, with batting-practice pitching instead of a live pitcher. I was playing center field at the time, and a teammate crushed one into the right center gap. I started sprinting toward the ball and realized about halfway there I had a shot at catching it if I dove. As I got closer, I leaped as far as I could, and to give me a few extra inches of room, I turned away from the ball, and surprisingly made the catch.

That was eight years ago, but I can still see it play out in slow motion in my head. Because of the awkward turn I took and the height at which I caught the ball, I came crashing to the ground with my right arm across my chest. I then heard one of the loudest pops I've ever heard in my life.

The pain was immediately searing, but I thought it'd wear off in a few seconds as a lot of injuries do. When I tried to get up, I literally couldn't move my arm. It just laid flat by my side while I was writhing back and forth on my knees. When the coach and a few others came to meet me out there, we realized just how serious it was. Because I couldn't move, they had to cut off my jersey to take a look. My collarbone was sticking out an inch or two from where it normally should be. I had completely shattered it.

My season was over. No more baseball. No more playing. No more shot at the state championship. I broke my collarbone so badly I had to get two metal plates and ten screws to put it back in place.

After that happened I had a lot of time to think because there isn't much to do in a hospital bed besides eat Jello and watch *The Price Is Right*. The weird part was that—even though it wasn't permanent, even though we didn't know for sure at the time—I lost a huge part of my identity in a flash.

I had been playing competitive baseball since I could remember. Thousands of dollars. Tons of equipment. Trainers. Trips. Time. Energy. Sweat. My life orbited around baseball. It was a pillar, a center of gravity, in my life.

And then, in a moment, it was gone.

It's human nature: we only notice the true value of something once it's gone. When baseball was taken from me, I realized I didn't just like it, I worshiped it. I was defined by it. I got my worth from it. It was my god, my functional savior.

Of course, I'd never have said that. But my life pointed to that.

Going back to the garden of Eden, we see humans were put in a unique space. We were below the Creator and above the creation. We were created in God's image, meaning we had a capacity no one else did. We had the weight of reflecting the very person who spun the earth into existence. He gave us that capacity.

The best way I've ever heard this explained is we are like mirrors slanted 45 degrees. We were created to stand in this middle place. God's glory, love, and likeness shine down on us, and like any slanted mirror should, we reflect that goodness and beauty out into the world.

It works backward too. As image-bearers, our job is to be gardeners as Adam was before he ate the fruit. We are to take raw materials, make something creative and beautiful, and then offer that to God as worship. A gardener shapes, cultivates, plants, and ultimately brings value to something that before had no value.

To take sounds of instruments and make music.

To take vegetables and herbs and make a beautiful meal.

To take paint and canvas and make art.

That's also the definition of a priest—someone who takes something and offers it as praise on behalf of others to God. Our job is to take the world, beauty out of chaos, and offer it back to God, as worship.

God in the garden called us to cultivate by holding that mirror at a 45-degree angle. It's a two-way thing. Something comes down and reflects out, and something comes from out and reflects up. When we reflect the beauty and goodness of the Creator out into the world, we are fulfilling this, and when we take the world and offer it through that mirror up to God, we are doing this as well.

But the minute Adam and Eve ate the fruit, that mirror shattered. It still might give a reflection of some sort, but we all know broken mirrors certainly don't give *accurate* reflections. We no longer reflect God, but are like broken shards of glass reflecting that very first sin: the desire to be like God. We reflect evil, chaos, power, greed, corruption, addiction.

And it can all be traced back to worship. When sin happened and the cosmos broke, a vacuum was created. Our life was in shalom. We were in a flourishing garden and earth with beauty, art, and amazing color. We were fully human. We knew God and walked with him in the garden. We were orbiting around God and everything he offers—goodness, beauty, peace, and rhythm.

But when the fracture happened, that center of ours became void. It got replaced. And like any good vacuum, stuff started getting sucked into that center. God was no longer in our hearts, so it was easy to let the first thing we came across take its place. We took the creation and elevated it above the creator. The very things we were created to dominate now dominate us. The things we were to create and cultivate now enslave us and rule us. The rule of the garden had been reversed. We no longer had dominion. We had slavery.

That is still happening today. Everything is vying for our attention. Everything is asking for our all: Sex. Beauty. Security. Athletics. Money. Self-worth.

Searching for these outside of God becomes our everything. Baseball wasn't my sport, it was my god—and there's a big difference.

That's the definition of an idol: something that promises to fulfill what only God truly can. It calls on our good desires—for love, intimacy, fullness, purpose—but then turns them from a good thing to a god thing. It puts the fulfillment of desire on a throne and then becomes our master.

WE ARE STATUES SENT FROM THE CAPITAL

When ancient capital cities are excavated, it is rare to find statues of whatever god or king ruled there. Rome, for example, hardly had any statues of Caesar. Most statues of rulers were found in the colonies, far away from the capital.

Statues, or images, are a way of saying who is in charge. Whether it's a huge statue or a face on a coin, the people know who is their lord when they see his face—even in a place he may never have visited. The statue set up in a colony one thousand miles from Rome is a way of saying Caesar is Lord. It serves as a reflection and reminder.

And so are we. We are living, breathing statues on earth as image-bearers of who is in charge. The problem, though, is that unlike statues, we can turn around and say no.

No, I don't want to worship you. No, I don't want to represent you. No, I don't want to reflect you. That's when the Bible says phrases like God "gave us over" to false gods, idols, and worship of the creation instead of the Creator.

There are two significant consequences every time we make that decision: (1) we are no longer able to properly reflect him, and (2) we become like the idols we worship.

Think about the statues again in the colonies. If for some reason Rome "gave up" on a colony and let it be, and it no longer maintenanced or cleaned the statues, they would deteriorate and crumble.

When they are cut off from the source, they don't realize they are cutting themselves off from the very thing that gives them their being. If Rome writes off a few statues and no longer takes care of them or "gives them over" to themselves, those statues quickly will no longer be representing Rome. They will simply be rubble and a pile of marble or stone.

When we decide to worship something besides God, that same thing happens with us. We begin to lose the thing that makes us human. Our humanness begins to crumble. As image-bearers we have weight, but when we abdicate that responsibility, we lose that weight. Our glory begins to fall. We become ruins of what he created us to be.

Now of course we never fully lose that image while we are alive. No matter how hard you scratch, gnaw, or pull, you can't get the image of God off of you fully. There's still glory residue no matter how hard you try. But the principle that is impossible to escape is we can't be image neutral—we *will* reflect or become more and more like something or someone.

When heaven crashes down onto earth, it looks like we are reflecting and imaging God's very own self in us. But to keep God from coming close, the only thing we have to do is worship something else as ultimate. Like the statue, it immediately cuts us off from the source and takes away our humanness.

It's a scary question but one that should be asked: What would you be like if the thing that made you human—the image and likeness of God—was taken away from you?

In C. S. Lewis's novel *The Great Divorce*, hell is painted as a picture of what happens when that image is fully removed. Heaven is inhabited by "solid people" and hell is inhabited by "ghosts." There is a weight in heaven that is so real, so thick, it's painful to the ghosts. In hell, they live hundreds of miles away from the nearest person. And hell is airy, thin, ghostlike. But heaven is dense, huge in proportion to hell. The bodies have weight, as if they were made for that place.

When the people in hell visit heaven, even the blades of grass are too dense to walk on. It's painful to them because they had been *dehumanized*. By wanting to worship themselves and other things, the very thing that made them truly human (namely God's reflected image in them) was scratched away. "Reality is harsh to the feet of shadows."[1] They don't have that image in them. They don't have that weight of glory. They are now sub-human. Sub-images.

And that's the logical conclusion of idolatry. It's colluding with evil to wipe away our humanness and to worship things that are not God. If we want to live our lives refusing the image of God in us, which is also the very thing that makes us human, hell becomes the place where God finally says okay. Which leads us to the second consequence: when God is no longer the image we orbit, then we become like whatever takes his place.

Either we worship God and become like him, or we worship something else and become like it. For example, when baseball was my life, I realized I subtly but surely became defined by my statistics. Baseball is a game of stats, and my very person began to be defined by those numbers. I wasn't a human regardless of how I played on the baseball field; I was whatever kind of day I had on the baseball field—worth nothing on a bad day, puffed up on a good day.

Another idol in my early life was sex. Porn took me down

this path of promise followed by despair—and from the immense amount of e-mails I get on this subject I know I'm not alone.

We might refer to ourselves as Christian or Muslim or Buddhist, but I'd argue that the biggest religion in the world is sexual fulfillment. We live in a society so entrenched, so addicted, it's blinding us.

Don't believe me?

- 2.5 billion e-mails per day are pornographic
- 1 out of every 4 search-engine requests is porn related
- *Sex* and *porn* are among the top 5 search terms for kids under 18
- 35 percent of *all* Internet downloads are pornographic.[2]

Sex is a god. And like any god, when you worship it, you become like it.

By the way, that knowledge is three thousand years old: "Those who make them become like them; / so do all who trust in them."[3]

Whatever you behold, you become like. Whatever you worship, you turn into. Whatever you turn your gaze to, it rubs off on you. Everything becomes colored by the idol. So many guys today don't see women as made in the image of God with inherent worth, dignity, and value. Instead, they see them as objects. They dehumanize them because of all the hours they spend on a computer screen watching their fantasies feed that lie. Women are simply there to satisfy men's desires. But little do they realize that when they dehumanize a girl, they, too, become hollow. Their humanness starts to decay. They become objects themselves. They erode their dignity, beauty, and the residue of God's image and become a pawn or commodity.

When you worship sex, you don't see humans, you see objects.

When you worship money, you don't see humans, you see transactions.

When you worship power, you don't see humans, you see pawns.

And in turn, you become like those things.

WE ALL WORSHIP SOMETHING

When I was at my non-Christian college, Jesus was fairly attractive to people in my circle. They enjoyed hearing about his grace and had no qualms about some of his teachings, but they usually got upset when they realized Jesus asked for everything.

When they'd see those passages about Jesus telling people to give up everything, say goodbye to all they know, they'd get upset.

How dare he. Who does he think he is?

They'd always freak out because they thought Jesus had no right to ask for everything from them. To put their whole lives, desires, and passions at his feet.

I never got why they *only* got mad at Jesus for that. Jesus isn't the only one who asks for everything. In fact, *everything* asks for everything.

Everything asks for your life. For your all. For every last drop of your allegiance.

Power does. Sexual fulfillment does. Athletics do. Your

significant other does. Your job does. Jesus isn't unique in that way. But he is unique in that he gave up everything first. All those other things use fear and false promises and force us to get what they want.

Jesus is the only one who lays his life down for you first, before he asks for yours. He pursues, he dies, he gives up everything and then calls us to himself. There's no force, only wooing. His love is so great that it *compels* us to lay down our lives in return. That's the only appropriate response when we understand just how great his sacrifice was for us.

God's heart in Psalm 115 tells us that he draws idolatry out to its logical conclusion: "Their idols are silver and gold, / the work of human hands. / They have mouths, but do not speak."⁴

God even makes the point that when we cry out to idols, they can't save us. They're dead. The paradox of an idol, unlike Jesus, is that the worshiper gives it power. We are the ones who give it life. Alcohol can only be a god if we make it one. Money can only be a god if we worship it. But Jesus is King and Lord regardless of what we do.

He's someone worth giving my life to.

Some of us instead still settle for idols, even though we don't realize it. We laugh at the imagery of the Old Testament as if we are more enlightened and would never do anything so foolish. Yet nothing has changed, except for the clothes the idols wear.

When's the last time that bottle of alcohol really satisfied? When's the last time it forgave you? Gave you joy? Fully loved you? It can't. We crafted it with our own hands.

What a lot of people don't realize is that an idol can be

anything. It can be good things like relationships or work. The problem is, even good things can become "god" things.

Young people are especially tempted to orbit their lives around significant others. Suddenly a switch flips in the heart, and we begin to get our satisfaction, worth, and identity from that person.

God is against idols because when the pieces of life are in their proper places, we can enjoy him and those things best. When we make another person an idol, we end up squeezing the life out of them. Only one person has the ability to sustain being God, and that's Jesus.

When we worship Jesus, we can love that person even more because our center isn't tied to or defined by them. If they upset us, rather than affecting us negatively every time, we can give back love, grace, and forgiveness because our self-worth comes from God.

It also doesn't work because people die. I heard a pastor say that one day when his wife dies, he will certainly grieve and be devastated, but he doesn't want to walk before the casket, and say, "There's my god. My god is dead." Being anchored in Jesus is the only way he'd be able to get through something like that.

Idols are fickle. Be it a person, alcohol, sex, anything—they all make for cruel gods. For me, baseball was a particularly unstable god. My average went up and down. My performance swayed. I had good days, and I had bad days. It was ruthless when I didn't perform, and easy when I did. Sounds a lot like the schizophrenic gods of ancient times that people always worried they would anger. Yet God is constant. Always forgiving. Always loving. Never changing.

One of the biggest traits of an idol is that we are blinded to it. It seems normal to us.

That's the allure and power of an idol—we usually don't know we have one unless it gets attacked or taken away. The easiest way to find an idol is to poke it. If it's an idol, it'll show its teeth. It'll bark back. They always do.

But Jesus doesn't need defending. He never defended himself but gave himself as an offering and in the process defeated evil (in a moment when everyone thought evil had won!).

Charles Spurgeon said it best: "The gospel is like a caged lion. It does not need to be defended, it just needs to be let out of its cage." The mystery of Jesus is just like the mystery in Revelation 5. He's *called* the Lion of Judah, but when John looks, he *sees* a lamb slaughtered. Jesus is a powerful, victorious lion who achieved that victory by the act of the lamb who was slain.

May we be people who, similar to the creatures around the throne in Revelation, worship the Lamb and sing his praise: "To him who sits on the throne and to the Lamb / be blessing and honor and glory and might forever and ever!"[5]

CHAPTER SEVEN

THE KINGDOM'S NOT WHERE YOU THINK

IT'S NOT IN THE SKY; IT'S HERE NOW

SON OF GOD.

King of kings.

Lord of lords.

Those were titles for a man who lived two thousand years ago. He was even called a savior because he was to bring peace to the world. He was divine and human, and they even argued that our calendars should revolve around him. The only problem is, this man is dead and so is his kingdom.

His name? Caesar Augustus.

Were you thinking of someone else?[1]

This was the atmosphere of the first century. All sorts of people were promising peace, order, and security; but only the Caesar had a right to do so. When Jesus declares he is Lord and he is King, the response was explosive, revolutionary, and offensive. Because if Jesus is King, that implies Caesar *is not*.

This royal kingly language would have been common to an everyday first-century person, and so it echoes and slips into a lot of the New Testament almost without our noticing it.

When reading the gospels it's pretty obvious that their sermons don't sound much like our sermons either; there aren't a lot of the gospel invitations so many of us are used to hearing every

Sunday. The way we usually present Jesus is something to the effect of, "Accept Jesus into your heart and you can go to heaven when you die."

Something I've really struggled with is when you read Acts, a book basically telling the power and struggles story of the Jesus movement right after he was resurrected, you never really see this version of the gospel at all. In all eight long sermons in Acts, no afterlife is even mentioned! It's all about the here and now. Jesus is the new emperor of the world, the apostles say, and we need to live accordingly.

But if we were to get into the DeLorean (shoutout to Marty again) and go back two thousand years and present our modern version of the gospel, no one would have any problem with it. You tell someone in the first century they need to accept Jesus and they can go to heaven when they die, they'd probably say, "Sure! That sounds great. Let's do it. It's the first century, baby. We're so tolerant."

No one had any qualms about telling people they can go to a better place when they die. And yet, Jesus followers were ridiculed, imprisoned, beaten, and in many cases, brutally murdered.

So in a pluralist society, why were Jesus followers treated as enemies of the state? Thrown to lions? Killed for sport? Squashed at all costs?

Asking people to accept Jesus into their hearts probably wouldn't have gotten anyone killed.

But three words did: *Jesus is Lord.*

If you're a twenty-first-century Westerner, this is especially hard to understand. We talk badly about our leaders all the time, and it's not really that big of a deal. It seems normal and smart, so we don't look like blind robots following them. But Rome, and antiquity in general, wasn't a republic. Dictatorships are all about giving allegiance to the highest power. If you don't, you can be beaten, tortured, or killed. Blasphemy was treason.

So when you read that phrase in the New Testament that says, "Jesus is Lord," don't imagine a nice Christian bookmark with that phrase. These were "fightin' words," as my mom likes to say. Because anytime you say, "Jesus is Lord," you are also saying,

"Caesar is not king,"

"Jupiter is not god,"

and "Money, sex, and power are not in control."

This little group of people was going around telling everyone that Jesus is King, Lord, and fully reigning and ruling and everything else was a parody. That claim was dangerous!

There is one God, not many. Jesus is King. And *that* is good news. That is gospel.

When we read the New Testament, the early church had two messages:

1. Jesus is Lord, and
2. The kingdom of heaven is near. Right after he describes Jesus' temptation in the desert, Matthew quotes Jesus as saying, "Repent, for the kingdom of heaven is at hand."[2]

Now, of course, that wasn't the only sentence Jesus uttered in his entire ministry, but Matthew is making the claim that this was one of the main thrusts of Jesus' message: The kingdom of heaven is near.

A kingdom is any place ruled by a king. It's a space of ruling, reigning, and governmental authority. Jesus is saying that God's kingdom—the place where God reigns and rules—has now crash landed in himself. He is the God of Israel, visiting his people and fulfilling the promise to establish his reign and rule in their midst.

Growing up, I always thought our hope was that we would get evacuated, that one day I would get snatched up into the sky and leave this nasty and evil earth. But from the very first sentence God seems to be about restoration. He doesn't want us to leave; he wants to come here himself. That God's reign and rule would be established in our finances, academics, sexuality, and jobs. That God would dwell with us.

One of my favorite movies is *Thor*. Thor is a god from another planet with immense strength and a huge battle-hammer. In both *Thor* movies, there is this move that Thor always does. When he's fighting, sometimes he will jump super high in the air, lift his hammer, and then come crashing down to the ground with the head of the hammer. Because of the weight and force, a crater is formed in the ground, and then there is this immense ripple force that basically knocks out everyone in its path.

I like to think the kingdom is like that. A lot of times we think the kingdom is something highly spiritual or fluffy. But it has a weight and a force to it, even if it was peaceful. Jesus' grace, mercy, and love were heavy. And when he unleashed them through his death and resurrection, there was a ripple. It was God himself saying, "I'm now in charge, and my reign is being ushered in." Anyone in his path couldn't help but get hit by the power of love, grace, and healing.

There is power in the kingdom.

One peculiar story in Matthew 8 describes a leper who comes and kneels before Jesus and says, "Lord, if you will, you can make me clean." In the Old Testament, leprosy was a ferocious skin disease that left anyone with it deeply marginalized. They were outcasts. Most people thought they must have done something wrong or God was upset at them for them to get sick.

Sadly, the church hasn't been too good at letting the inclusive kingdom call ring true. I've been to churches in Europe where there were little one-inch slits on the outside of the building where the lower class or marginalized or "unclean" people could watch the service without coming in and infecting everyone else.

But what's crazy about the story in Matthew 8 is that Jesus reaches out and *touches* the man. This man was a leper! Any Jew would have known that touch would have made himself ceremonially unclean, according to the priests.

But this rabbi reaches out and touches him. And in a split second, the cleanest person in the world and in all history chooses to collide with someone who is unclean. And guess what happens? Jesus wins. It says upon Jesus' touch "immediately his leprosy was cleansed."[3]

This was scandalous because up until that time, uncleanness always won. For the first time, the clean infects the unclean. There is a force, an energy, a holiness about Jesus that emanates off of him and into anyone who touches him. That is the kingdom. There's power being unleashed, and God's reign is breaking forth in the midst of the old creation.

The good news of the Bible is that when you step into God's kingdom and under his authority, everything changes.

Sometimes people think Christianity is a take it or leave it option. Meaning, we can accept Jesus or not, but the choice doesn't really change much. When you understand the power of the statement "Jesus is Lord," you realize that how we respond to that kingdom call is of the greatest importance. And then as kingdom people wherever we go, the power of the kingdom goes with us. Who is our king? Are we bowing to something else?

Imagine it's the first century, and you're living in a state that's about to be colonized by Rome. As usual the empire would send a herald of some sort who would come with a scroll in hand to shout to the town that under decree of Caesar, "It is now announced that he is in charge of your town. He is the new governmental authority."

Now what it probably didn't look like was this herald coming and saying, "All right everyone, Caesar is the new lord, but honestly you don't have to really restructure your life around that truth. It's a take it or leave it type of thing. If you want to make Caesar your lord, maybe come back next week for an informational meeting and we'll tell you how to do that."

We know that's laughable, because that's not what kings do. Caesar was lord *regardless* of how the new colony acted. Either they stepped into that truth, or they were rebels.

The declaration of Jesus is basically the same as Caesar's, but even better since it's the real thing. Jesus as Lord is the best news in the world, and we can step into that truth or become rebels. Except instead of killing us if we don't obey, we don't realize we are rebelling against the ability to know true love.

This Jesus, who died for his enemies and inaugurated his new world in the resurrection, is love (that's what 1 John says about God: He is love). That means we are rebels if we say no, but saying no is saying no to love, to what it means to be human, to flourishing, and to all the beauty and grace and forgiveness that marks the kingdom of God. We are like starving people saying no to bread simply because we don't want to receive a "handout."

But if we say yes to the beautiful call that the kingdom is near, our journey begins. The minute we say yes to Jesus as King, our kingdom collides with his.

During college I'd often stay up until at least three in the morning, go to class dead tired, and then catch up on sleep in the middle of the day. I kept my dorm pretty orderly, but not necessarily clean. Meaning, I like everything to be in its right place but am not too concerned about everything being deep cleaned too often. College was a time of doing things how I liked it, doing things my way and organizing my life around my own rhythms and patterns.

All that changed when Alyssa and I got married. When we stood at the altar, we were colliding our kingdoms. Our domains, the ways we governed ourselves, now had to be restructured and reordered. We had to start over. We had to reorient and reorbit around our identity as a married couple.

The problem though is, it's not that easy. In fact, you realize how much of your own kingdom you have once you get married.

You think you're not selfish? You don't think you're impatient? You think you're "flexible"? I did. Until I got married. If you're not married yet, by the way, just wait until the second day of your marriage when you argue about where the trash can goes, which way the toilet paper rolls, among many other things.

Alyssa and I were learning a new way of life. Being legally married wasn't the goal. That's the title. True marriage is two lives meshing and colliding until piece by piece and moment by moment we continually are becoming one new person.

A lot of Christians, though, settle for only the title. When we enter into a relationship with Jesus, we become Christians. We receive that title and identity in the same way when I entered into a relationship with Alyssa I became married.

It didn't take long to realize just how selfish I was, just how hurtful I could be with snarky comments, and just how unfocused I could be as a leader and servant. It's only when we clash with another kingdom, or a new way of life, that we realize how poor the one before truly was.

For example, one of the things Alyssa quickly exposed is the fact that I can sometimes be argumentative. But Alyssa has gently reminded and showed me that there is more joy and life operates better when I purposefully take a listening posture. It was only when her sweetness, kindness, and all-around gentleness exposed me that I saw that. If I had thought getting married was the end of the road, not the beginning, I never would have cared to make those changes in myself.

Many of us think that when we start following Jesus, that's the end. We want the wedding, but we don't want the marriage.

When, in fact, saying yes to Jesus is the beginning. Just as we do in marriage, we are to reorbit, reorient, and come under God's reign and rule and his way of doing things.

Life isn't about going to heaven when you die, it's about making heaven true on earth in every facet and level of our relationship with God, others, and self. The Christian life is asking, how can I make what's true of Jesus and his gospel true in whatever aspect of my life?

For something to be a kingdom, there must be a king, kingdom citizens, and a governing structure or way of life. A lot of us have the first two, not realizing the last one comes with it. We take Jesus as our savior, we become citizens of his kingdom, but we fail to realize that for that to be true, our lives now have to come under his reign.

The people of Israel had this. God was King, the Israelites were citizens, and the Law was the way of life. Then it shouldn't be lost on us—that was exactly what Matthew was trying to say about the Sermon on the Mount. In it, Jesus absorbed the Law into himself and then put a radical spin on it that is now the new way of living and being human. It was Law and Moses 2.0.

Jesus not only goes up on a hill, similar to Moses going up on the mountain, but then begins the first of five extremely large chunks of teaching by Jesus in the entire book of Matthew. And reading the book of Matthew, it's apparent that the five huge chunks of teaching is an allusion to Israel's first five books of the Bible, the Torah. He's saying quite clearly that Jesus is the *new* Torah. And he's not abolishing the old Torah, he's fulfilling it and reshaping it and bringing it deeper.

He's explosively saying that those who trust in Jesus are the new Israel (children of Abraham), and Jesus' teachings are the governing authority or structure that should define the people as kingdom citizens.

I remember spending some time in Uganda a few years ago and being immediately struck with how quickly I stood out. Of course, my skin color was a huge part of this, but so was my way of life. For example, we'd have church services with the local workers and staff of the orphanage where we were staying, and it was quite apparent who was a local and who was a Mzungu (white person, usually from America) by who danced and who didn't in their worship—they clap, dance, and shout; and we in the West are quite reserved.

But I stand out in other Western countries too. Alyssa and I were in Europe a few years ago, and I remember sitting at a dinner table waiting for our check for an incredible length of time. I thought the restaurant had horrible service, and I was contemplating tipping poorly, when we were informed that in Europe it's rude for the server to bring the check before asked. It was clear from how we were behaving that we were American.

There were markers or things that made us stand out. Our culture and citizenship made us look different from the native people.

That's what it means to be in the kingdom. To put our whole lives under God's reign, and live as a new humanity, a community that points to the future of the restoration of all things.

What are those things that make us stand out? What is our charter? What do we need to change to become full citizens of God's kingdom?

THE LAST SHALL BE FIRST

It was a Sunday afternoon right after I'd finished speaking to a youth group. The youth pastor and his wife were asking us to lunch after the service, but I quickly jumped in and said no. Alyssa then gave me that look. Why can't we go out to lunch with them? I couldn't really produce a good reason, except that Alyssa and I had already planned to picnic that day.

The truth was, I intended to propose to her in just a couple of hours.

I still remember the moment. I had two of my buddies go ahead of me to the location—a nice little private beach area over-looking the Puget Sound. I had them go a few hours before to set up everything. I printed out every picture we had ever taken in our relationship and had one of them post those on the fence leading down to the beach, along with rose petals and candles. My other buddy set up a couple of cameras too. (I'm a YouTuber—I have to record everything.) I felt like a secret service agent: I even had a microphone taped under my shirt the whole time.

I had this grand picture in my mind, but when I got to the moment, I was so awkward. I had all this stuff I wanted to say, but literally could barely get any of it out. I think it's the only time in my life when I've been at a loss for words and stumbled through sentences I'm not even sure were English.

One thing I did was read a journal entry "to my future wife" that I'd written a couple of years before and told Alyssa I believed that was her. Then I got out a thermos of hot water and a bowl and proceeded to wash Alyssa's feet.

It sounds sweet, but honestly it was kind of awkward. Do I just kind of take the washcloth and rub her feet? Do I get in the nooks and crannies and make sure they are totally clean? Is my washing them telling her that her feet are dirty and they need cleaning?

In reality, when I was washing her feet, I told her I wanted this to be a symbol of our relationship. I wanted to serve her, love her, and cherish her. It was a moment I won't forget.

But I haven't always kept that promise. There are times I'm selfish, impatient, and unloving, and I have to return again and again to that feet washing. That service. That love.

Functionally, foot washing made a lot more sense in first-century Palestine since everyone was usually wearing retro Birkenstocks. Their feet would get filthy from the dust and whatever else was left scattered on paths and streets.

Because of the nature of foot washing, especially in a Jewish culture of daily and ritual cleanliness, it was even beneath Jewish slaves to wash someone's feet. Most prominent Jews had a slave at the door who would untie your sandals, but it was usually reserved for the person himself to wash his own feet with water provided by the host.

So you can see just how lowly and scandalous Jesus' actions are in John 13. Toward the end of his life, he was having a meal with his disciples and then took off his outer garments, tied a towel around his waist, poured water into a basin, and began to wash his disciples' feet.[4]

That'd be like the president of the United States taking off his suit, getting on his hands and knees, and washing your feet after a long hike in the mountains. It would feel weird and almost inappropriate. We probably would have reacted the same way Peter did and refuse it.

But Jesus insists. He even goes on to tell Peter that if he doesn't let him wash Peter's feet, then Peter has no part in him. When Jesus was done, he said, "A servant is not greater than his master, nor is a messenger greater than the one who sent him."[5]

I think washing someone's feet holds the same shock value today as it did two thousand years ago, and so we shouldn't be afraid to do it from time to time for friends, enemies, and in moments where we want to disturb and disrupt people to ask us about Jesus. But I also think foot washing can be metaphorical.

Essentially, it's serving. It's taking the lowest seat and doing what others won't. Jesus clearly states that the kingdom operates and sees power differently than the world. According to Jesus, the "powerful" are the servants. The ones who make themselves last.

I'm challenged to live this out every day of my marriage. For twenty-three years I was conditioned to see that life was about my priorities, my goals, and the other details of my life. Yet Jesus strangely says if we want to find our lives and find joy, we have to lose them. We have to give them up. There are moments, I wish more often, when I sit and rest in Jesus and am able to turn to Alyssa and serve her.

For the longest time, we argued over making the bed. To Alyssa it's what starts the day and makes the day feel right. It gives a joy and attitude about the day. For me, I think it's ridiculous because I have a tough time doing something I know will get messed up every twenty-four hours for the rest of my life.

But I finally decided to put my arguments aside and simply serve Alyssa. Even though it's something really small, I understand what Jesus was talking about. There's this strange joy that begins to come. After I make the bed, I do admit it looks nice, but more important, it does something for Alyssa. She feels loved, cherished, and valued. It creates this dynamic and spirit about our relationship that fills us, gives us joy, and brings us just a tiny bit closer together.

It even produces this dance-like rhythm in our marriage in which we are mutually serving and dancing with each other in love. And if you've been in that spot, you know that's the spot we were created for. That's the kingdom.

What could you do today or tomorrow that hoists the kingdom flag of serving? I think drastic things specifically have a way of shocking people out of their worldview and making them even for a second, ask, why? We talk a lot about Jesus, but if we washed some more feet, more people might start following him.

What would it look like if you tried to think of something creative that could serve your peers or friends? If you're in a college, maybe knock on dorm rooms and ask them if you can do a load of their laundry. Sounds absurd, but can you imagine what a person would think if you asked that? That moment might stick with them for years, and it took you maybe twenty minutes. (Warning: if it's a freshman guy's clothes, you might need a biohazard suit.)

The best part about Jesus and his kingdom is it's *creative*. He spits in the mud, rubs it on his hands, smears in on a guy's eyes, and the man's healed.

He tells Peter, "Hey, go look in that fish's mouth. There will be money."

Don't be afraid to be creative in serving others, because it just might show them a little sparkle of what Jesus is like, and they'll then check out the source.

THE SWORD OR THE CROSS

One thing that stood in stark contrast to Rome was that the kingdom of Jesus seemed to think self-giving love could conquer enemies, while Rome thought, killing that enemy will do the trick.

It's hard to read the New Testament and not think America looks a lot more like the empire of Rome than the kingdom of Jesus. I agree with N. T. Wright: "When God wants to change the world, he doesn't send in the tanks. He sends in the meek, the mourners, those who are hungry and thirsty for God's justice, the peacemakers, and so on."[6]

Did you know the Pentagon spends more on war than all fifty states spend on health, education, welfare, and safety combined? As a country we spend more on our military than the next fifteen countries combined.[7]

If we are to be people of the light, we should study history. Looking back it's easy to see the empire that thought it could get what it wanted by killing people doesn't exist anymore. The kingdom that thought it could transform people's lives by loving them still exists—and is growing.

And some might say, "Well, Jesus' world was different than ours." To which I'd answer, "You're right; it was way worse."

The Jewish people technically had been back from exile for almost five hundred years by the time of Jesus. They were in their own land. Yet for almost that entire period, outside of a few blips on the radar, the Persian, Greek, or Roman empires ruled them all but about twenty-five of those years. For the Jewish people, this indicated something deeply wrong. God had promised to establish his reign and rule and do something new and explosive in Israel. If Cyrus or Alexander the Great or Caesar were still ruling Judea, then that meant it hadn't happened yet.

The Jewish people were anxiously waiting for a leader to rise up. To do what they had read about in the Prophets: crush the enemies, defeat the occupying country, and establish Israel as its own sovereign nation again.

When was God going to establish his kingdom for Israel and the faithful?

Little did they know he was about to do that very thing, but in a radically different way than anyone expected.

A lot of people figured this would happen through—you guessed it—physical violence. That's how it happened in the Old Testament, and that's how Judas Maccabeus attempted it two hundred years earlier. Because that's simply the only way to get rid of a foreign occupier.

And yet Jesus radically opposed that violence. In fact, in every instance that killing the enemy becomes a viable option for the followers of Jesus in the gospels, Jesus flatly condemns it.

When Peter cuts off a man's ear to protect Jesus, he's rebuked harshly.

When Jesus triumphantly enters Jerusalem, he cries because Jerusalem didn't know the things "that make for peace."[8]

When Jesus is arrested and taken to a Roman execution device, he seems to give up no fight.

When two disciples asked to be placed at his left and right in his kingdom (they thought Jesus was going to violently take the temple back and establish his earthly rule), he says they clearly do not know what they are asking.

It was clear by the fact he was gaining and attracting such large crowds that people thought God's long-awaited promise to crush Rome and establish Israel forever was coming true in Jesus. And so Jesus very quickly goes right to the people's hearts.

He puts his cards on the table in the very first sermon in Matthew, famously called the Sermon on the Mount. Which, by the way, as we've already seen previously, wasn't just potent teaching, but set up by Matthew to tell the reader, "This is the new Torah! This is the new Law! This is the manifesto for Jesus followers!" It wasn't just a nice teaching that we can put on a coffee cup but something we are responsible to live out if we call ourselves Jesus followers.

Jesus explicitly addresses the Old Testament way of doing things: "You have heard that it was said, 'You shall love your neighbor and hate your enemy.' But I say to you, Love your enemies and pray for those who persecute you, so that you may be sons of your Father who is in heaven."[9]

Jesus is saying, "I know you've heard it a certain way. I know you think that way is right. But if you want to be a part of this movement turning the world upside down and living in my king-dom, then you need to love your enemies." He even goes so far to say if someone slaps you, turn the other cheek. If they take your tunic, give them your cloak.

To really sit in just how dangerous this would've sounded to any first-century ears, think about this—remember how you felt on September 11, 2001? The shock, the ache, the pain, the anger? Now imagine it wasn't just the World Trade Center towers but the White House too. The very symbol of our nation.

Now try to imagine that those responsible for September 11 had ruled America for the previous century, and before that some other empires had ruled us. Imagine we were kept from doing the very things that made us American—the republic was completely squashed, capitalism and entrepreneurship were condemned, people by and large were not free.[10]

There was oppression, your siblings and family were being killed without consequences, and there were other brutal conditions that made living incredibly terrible. Everyone, no matter what they believed, had to give allegiance to Allah.[11] There was no religious freedom as we pride ourselves on in the Constitution. If people were out of line, they'd be killed or imprisoned.

What would be your response to this? Most likely, especially if in true American spirit, we'd do anything in our power to take down the force occupying us. We'd wait for any opportunities to defeat the evil guys occupying our country and land. To reclaim America and reestablish its beauty, honor, democracy, and patriotism.

We'd have visions of taking back the White House and raising the American flag on the front lawn. Our hope, though, if we're honest, starts to become dismal realizing that for twelve generations nothing has changed, and we haven't been able to get our country back.

Then let's imagine a leader comes along and says, "Instead of taking back America, instead of staging a coup, instead of taking down the enemies, love them. Forgive them. Wash their feet. Bless them—and if it calls for it, die for them. Even if they've killed your family and friends, and have made your entire life a nightmare."

Not only would that be offensive, it'd probably deeply anger a lot of us. Doesn't that leader know the pain, ache, grief, and oppression this regime has caused? Then let's imagine that leader causes quite a stir in saying all this, and in turn is arrested and then brutally tortured in Times Square on camera for the entire nation to see. And at the end of the torture, he is hung and executed.

Hope is squashed and this leader who brought us the hope of getting our country back is publicly executed, which would've clearly meant it was a failure. His plan obviously didn't work. Yet a couple of weeks later something strange happens. A small group of people claim he came back to life a few days after he died and the very minute he was killed was actually, peculiarly, and mysteriously the answer to everyone's problems and, in fact, is the very event that will save and restore the entire world.

That is how ridiculous the cross looked to any faithful Jew living in Israel in the first century. Rather than being the moment of victory, the cross proved the very opposite! A crucified Messiah isn't a Messiah at all. All the hopes of Jesus restoring the kingdom of Israel were crushed the minute the Romans drove nails into his wrists and feet. All the followers of Jesus thought they had wasted the past three years of their lives.

Israel was occupied for so long they almost couldn't remember what it meant to be in their own land without anyone else running the show. Yet, in that moment love strangely won. Jesus, even in the middle of the execution, says while on the cross, "Father forgive them for they know not what they do."

Jesus could have easily crushed the opposition. He could have easily called down an army of angels to absolutely slaughter everyone who oppressed and hurt Israel. Instead he knew the way to change the world was through sacrificing his own life—and he calls us to do the same. That's a strong task and a strong call, but if we are Jesus followers, that's the path carved for us. Sacrificial love, giving one's life on behalf of another, is the way of our Lord and must be our way too. It's one of the most defining marks of a Jesus-kingdom citizen.

As pastor Brian Zahnd put it, "Ultimately we cannot eliminate enemies through violence—violence only multiplies enemies. The only way to eliminate enemies is to love them, forgive them."[12]

This isn't just a nice concept. It's intensely pertinent right now since ISIS (Islamic State of Iraq and Syria) is all over the news for brutal and grotesque violence in some regions of Iraq and Syria. They are going on a graphic conquest destroying anything that doesn't line up with their vision for the world. Beheadings are being shown on TV and the Internet; daughters are being raped; people are being sold as slaves.

Just reading about some of the actions of the group made me physically ill. Barbaric, grotesque, and brutal actions. Hundreds of thousands of people in the area have been displaced, hurt, abandoned, and are on the run. I ache for my brothers and sisters there.

One thing that is particularly painful is how I'm afraid we will only stand with them as long as the news cycle lasts. But if we are Jesus followers, we stand against such atrocity not for two weeks, but for good. We use our lives and our means to say no. That is not okay, and God is not pleased. Jesus is God's answer to evil, and it must be ours too.

All throughout history God has creatively curbed evil and brought about justice.

A beautiful symbol of this is the *Tree of Life* in the British Museum where assault rifles and machine guns used in the Mozambique civil war were taken by authorities in exchange for shovels, sewing machines, and even a tractor. Four war survivors broke the weapons and formed a tree depicting life. Forgiveness. New start. Peace.

It's a perfect representation of God's heart declared in Isaiah: "He will judge between the nations and will settle disputes for many peoples. They will beat their swords into plowshares and their spears into pruning hooks. Nation will not take up sword against nation, nor will they train for war anymore."[13]

One thing that's even harder to imagine, though, is if ISIS was in control of where I live. What if those atrocities were happening right now in the middle of our country?

What if you could defeat this evil? Completely crush it. Show it for what it is—evil that does not belong in this world or God's plans. Would you? Of course. But let's take it another step further.

Ultimately we know if all of ISIS is killed, another group sooner or later will rise up. So what if, instead of just defeating ISIS, you could defeat evil itself? What if the force, the spirit, the evil behind all tangible evil could be destroyed? Would you? Of course you would.

The truth is, that's already happened, according to claims of a first-century rabbi in Judea. And he said it's already happened, get this, when he was executed by the Romans and resurrected three days later.

That is the most explosive, countercultural, ridiculous thing I've ever heard. Jesus said he defeated evil in a six-hour event that left him in agony, bloodied to a pulp, and dangling from a piece of wood. That's the foolishness of the cross Paul talks about in 1 Corinthians.

And if Jesus said that and modeled that, the question becomes, do we really trust him that the Jesus way is the way?

For thousands of years Jesus followers have altered history, changed cultures, and left lasting legacies simply because they believed this to be true.

When they were thrown to lions and had their bodies ripped—no chewed—apart, they bled love not hatred.

When Peter was crucified, he didn't pull out the sword as he did on the night of Jesus' arrest; he asked to be crucified upside down because he wasn't worthy of dying in the same way as his Lord.

I read about a Christian man who heard guards coming to his door to arrest him and take him to his execution. He quickly greeted them and asked if he could cook them a warm meal since they had traveled all that way, and then they could take him.

Enemy love changes the world. Enemy love breaks and transforms hearts. Enemy love makes people look to Jesus. And enemy love is nonnegotiable in the kingdom.

This topic brings up loads of practical questions that space here won't allow, and also because I don't know the answers to a lot of those questions. But the big question is, are we even having this conversation? Are we wrestling?

This concept isn't one that's nice and tidy. It deserves creative solutions. I'm learning day by day to really trust that Jesus knew what he was doing. He can be trusted. His way is the way of the future like we talked about in chapter 4.

It is foolishness to the world, but somehow the mysterious heart of God says this is the way, and looking back on church history, time and time again radical love does defeat evil.

THANKFULNESS IS THE SECRET

Foot washing and enemy love aren't the only markers of a kingdom citizen. Thankfulness, too, is a badge that should mark us as Jesus followers.

For the longest time I thought God wanted me to do something super-spiritual for him if I was going to follow him and do "big" things. I believed in order for God to really like me, I needed to do something crazy for him, such as move to Africa or heal cancer.

But the apostle Paul, on multiple occasions, says stuff like, "And whatever you do, in word or deed, do everything in the name of the Lord Jesus, giving thanks to God the Father through him."[14]

Or to Timothy he says, "For everything created by God is good, and nothing is to be rejected if it is received with thanksgiving, for it is made holy by the word of God and prayer."[15]

In another place he even says to give thanks in all circumstances.[16]

I think thanksgiving is the secret to a healthy Christian life. When we feel as if we earned something, we become entitled and smug. But if we understand even the oxygen in our lungs is a gift from an amazing and beautiful Creator, then gratitude and thankfulness start to explode in our lives. When we can be thankful, we get joy.

Author Ann Voskamp has written beautifully about the art of thanksgiving in her book *One Thousand Gifts*. She kept a running list of everything she was thankful for, big and small, and she noticed it unlocked something in her heart.

The best part about thanksgiving is we can do it anywhere. I thought I had to do big things for God, but when I started to really read the New Testament, I realized God wasn't as concerned with me doing big things as he was with my attitude in the middle of the thing I was already in. I didn't have to be a pastor or a theologian to be more holy. Holiness happens when thanksgiving happens, and I can do that if I'm typing, writing, cooking, walking, or playing sports.

What if you took your life as it is now, and rather than thinking you have to do something more spiritual or holy, just infuse a ton of thanksgiving right there in the middle of it?

Thanksgiving has also been a way to show what things I should do and what things I should steer clear from. It's a lot easier to know what might be a sinful or poor decision in my life when I can't give thanks for it.

I can't thank God that I stole a car, and I can't thank God when I lie to a friend because I know those aren't things he orchestrated or provided. If you can't give thanks for something, then that's a good sign you probably shouldn't be doing it.

And the question we always have to ask is, *what's it like in heaven right now and how do I make this true on earth?*

In Scripture we see heaven isn't far away; it's simply God's dimension. His space. Isaiah, the Gospels, and Revelation give us a peek behind the curtain, where we see worship and thanksgiving. Thanking God for what he's done, what he's doing, and what he's about to do. And in that moment when we are thankful to and worship him, we fulfill the very core of the kingdom prayer.

Growing up, I often heard the Lord's Prayer recited, and for some reason it always sounded as if people were reading it at a funeral—dry, dead, and monotone.

Yet at the center of the prayer, it says, "Your kingdom come, your will be done, on earth as it is in heaven."

Jewish folks in Jesus' day would bring emphasis to something by describing the same thing two different ways. Scholars argue that's what is going on: your kingdom come, your will be done. So where is God's kingdom coming? Simple: anywhere his will is being done.

And notice again how Jesus is teaching his followers to pray that the kingdom would come. Not leave, but come. Right here. Right now. In our midst.

And then it says, "on earth as it is in heaven." Make true on earth what is true in heaven.

Death isn't true in heaven, so we should be people of life here.

There's no bitterness in heaven, so we should forgive people here.

There's only a beautiful flourishing life in heaven, so we should make that happen here.

What if we really took that prayer to heart? What if we really believed it? What if we prayed it every morning?

I hung a wood-pallet art piece right above my computer to remind me: "Your kingdom come, your will be done, on earth as it is in heaven." I want that prayer to be at the forefront of my mind. When I see evil, I want to pray that his kingdom would come. When I see hurt, I want to pray that his kingdom would come.

One little exercise I've started doing recently is replacing the word *earth* with the city I live in: "Your kingdom come your will be done, in Kihei as it is in heaven." That makes it so much more real to me. The fun part is it makes me restudy the Bible and ask, how do I do this? What does heaven look like? What does God's space and dimension look like? What does the reign of Jesus look like, and how can I make that come by the power of the Spirit here in my city?

Do you pray that prayer? Do you have that heart for your city? What would it look like if you prayed that God's kingdom would exist in New York as it does in heaven? If you made that the cry of your heart?

CHAPTER EIGHT

BROKENNESS IS NOT WHAT YOU THINK

YOU MUST EMBRACE YOUR SCARS

I HAD JUST MOVED IN WITH MY AUNT AND UNCLE WHILE attending community college, and I was sitting on their couch about midday, ugly-face crying. If you've done the same, you know what I'm talking about. It's where a cry session turns the corner and becomes a full-blown weep.

I was really struggling at that time with a bunch of things—depression, things I'd done wrong, disenchantment and disillusionment with this whole Jesus-following thing. I finally broke and shared all the hurt, pain, and ache I had been holding onto.

It was the first time I had been really honest and taken off my mask. Whether it was friends asking how I was doing and always answering with the cliché "fine," or those dark thoughts I always had of *if people knew the real me, they'd run as fast as they could in the opposite direction*, I constantly played the game of projecting a certain version of myself.

I can't describe the sense of freedom I had when weights fell off my shoulders in that moment. I remember my aunt and uncle just listening, encouraging, and reminding me how much God loved me. It was truly healing.

We all have wounds—things that make us physically cringe just thinking about them. They could have been caused by something we've done or something that's been done against us; regardless, emotional wounds are sensitive.

For me, there are all the poor choices I made in high school and college that to this day haunt me when I'm not focusing on grace and Jesus. Or memories of growing up in a household with only one parent, when most of my friends had traditional families. Or tough breakups that give you that sense of searing pain that not much else does.

The problem with wounds, though, is that our first inclination is to cover them. We think if we just slap a bandage on, it'll heal by itself. And sometimes that might be true, but when it's a really bad wound, that only makes it worse. No one can see it, but it's festering. If left untreated, a covered wound can get an infection, which, if bad enough, could even kill you. Oxygen and daylight are some of the first steps to healing a wound.

What if that's what it's like when we don't deal with the wounds in our hearts? Nelson Mandela reminded us, "Resentment is like drinking poison and then hoping it will kill your enemies." Resentment or bitterness is a symptom of a spiritual wound. We get angry. We lash out. If you touch a wound, people coil back and cringe because it's so sensitive.

What would someone have to touch in your life for you to react like that? To recoil? To cringe?

What if God wants to heal that? What if he wants to turn your wounds into scars?

The interesting thing about scars is that we don't hide scars as we do wounds. Wounds we cover, we mask, we make sure no one can see or touch. Scars are the opposite. We aren't afraid to show our scars because they tell a story.[1]

I have a little tiny scar on my upper lip because I thought it'd be a great idea to eat a dog's food when I was a year old. The dog didn't think it was so genius, and he bit me in the face.

And as I mentioned earlier, I also have a six-inch scar on my right shoulder, with two titanium plates and ten screws inside, from when I shattered my collarbone diving for a baseball.

I have a one-inch clean scar on my right knuckle. I found my mom's pocketknife as a kid, took it into a hiding place, and began playing with it. Of course, I wasn't too sure what it did so I tested it on my pointer finger. It sliced me right open.

Scars tell stories. And for the most part, if people see a scar, they ask about it, and we are not afraid to tell them. Because they don't hurt anymore. You can touch any of my scars, and they don't hurt; I don't cringe or pull back. It's just an opportunity for me to tell you what happened and how it's been healed.

What if Jesus wants to take our wounds and turn them into scars? We don't have to be ashamed of them anymore. We can bring them to the Healer (a name God calls himself in Exodus 15:26).

Sometimes, though, it's not that easy. Some wounds get healed the minute we come to Jesus, while others are a lot harder to walk through.

About two years ago, Alyssa and I moved out of the city and into a smaller town close to the mountains. This town is only ten minutes away from where I went to high school, so we went there pretty often for groceries and Starbucks (of course).

Sometimes it is difficult for me to drive through that town without cringing on certain streets or near certain landmarks:

That was the park where I got high with my friends late at night.

That was the parking lot where I did things I'm ashamed of.

That is the street where a huge brawl almost broke out.

And on and on and on.

It's really hard for me to drive down those streets in that area because they remind me of a time in my life that I'm not proud of and when I didn't make the best decisions. It feels as if old wounds open and a lot of ache, grief, regret, and guilt just flood over me. Part of me gets upset and begins an internal dialogue.

I thought I was healed from all these things?

If I'm healed, why does it feel so vivid?

If there's grace for me, why do I feel so much guilt right now?

And it's in those moments I have to remember two things.

First, I can't buy the lie that God doesn't care or is aloof in those moments. He's not distant or far away. He's right there in the middle of the guilt, revolting thoughts, and self-condemnation. He's whispering.

But I also can't buy the lie of the other whisper.

As author Ann Voskamp put it, "The one hissed in the garden to Eve, the first deception that deceives us still—that God doesn't care about the needs of His children. And maybe this is why the world hemorrhages—if we think God doesn't care—why should we? Isn't it easier to blame Him? When I believe the Edenic lie that God doesn't care—is that the excuse to turn away, to spread the lie that God doesn't care—when maybe the truth is that it's humanity that doesn't care?"[2]

He's there. He knows. He heals. He comes close.

Second, I have to remind myself that past mistakes are not the truest things about me. It's just phantom pain. Someone who has lost an arm, leg, or some part of his body might have experienced *phantom pain*. It's when you feel sharp pain in a part of your body you don't even have anymore.

This phantom pain is not real even though brain synapses are firing and telling the person it is. I can't imagine how hard in that moment it is to believe it isn't real, even when you're able to look down and see you have no left foot. The pain is so sharp and vivid. But at the end of the day, the pain is simply not true.

I think that's a lot like what we feel in those regretful moments. When the same sin or same grief or same guilt keeps replaying, or when we drive by something that reminds us of it, or see something on Facebook that shoots a sharp guilt pain through our bodies, we have to remind ourselves that's phantom pain. It's not real. It's not the truest thing about us. In God's dimension, heaven, he has declared that when we follow him we are new. We are clean. We are forgiven. We are his children. He delights over us. He isn't distant, but near.

And *those* are the truest things about us. Not the voice of the wound. We can put our feet down in that moment, cry out for help, hang on tightly, and keep reminding ourselves that's not real. It's a scar. It's been healed.

Jesus says so, and we can trust him because he's been there.

He knows what it's like to be hurt, bruised, and beaten, and to ache. He knows what it's like to be betrayed and abandoned. He knows what it's like to give only love but receive only hate. He knows what it's like, and no other god can claim that.

Are you letting Jesus turn your wounds into scars? What if Jesus wants to heal the dark parts in your life, so then you can turn around and tell others just how good he really is? Only when a wound is a scar will we let it tell a story. You can then point at the scar and say, "Look what Jesus did."

In Japanese culture there is a type of pottery art called *kintsugi* that deals with broken items such as clay pots, vases, and bowls. When a bowl or pot breaks, *kintsugi* artists put it back together using a lacquer mixed with either gold, silver, or platinum.

When the pot is put back together, the gold, silver, or platinum veins running through the pot exactly where it had previously been broken are the most eye-catching. The new glory of the beautiful creation is the golden-laced broken pieces that have been repaired. If you google this art form you'll see what I'm talking about—it's remarkably beautiful.

With *kintsugi*, when something becomes broken, it doesn't become less valuable. The new golden-laced repair makes it *more* valuable. It doesn't try to hide or disguise the imperfections, but instead puts them on full display in all their beauty and glory.

I don't think we are much different when we come to Jesus. Some of the most inspiring people we know are those who have been hurt, broken, suffered, and yet still have a peace, joy, and resilience about them. Scars don't hide our history; they show it. And when we show our scars, we get to point to the healer

who wove his grace right into the depths of every crack and frag-
mented part in our soul.

Sometimes it's metaphorical scars, but sometimes it's physical
scars. I've talked to a lot of people who have tried for years to rid
themselves of shame and guilt and ache by cutting themselves.
I recently talked with someone who said she cuts because "she
thinks she deserves the pain."

My heart breaks when I hear that. The beauty of Jesus is that
he's not asking us to hurt ourselves, inflict pain, or make ourselves
worthy of him. We are already worthy because of who made us.
We have inherent value because the very Creator of the universe
spun us into existence, and he even rejoices over us![3] Thinking
we have to punish ourselves to be loved is nowhere in the Bible.
In fact, the opposite is claimed in the Bible.

Jesus took our pain on himself. He felt that weight, that crush-
ing sense of ache and pain, and he bore it fully. If pain and shame
were a cup, he drank it to the very last drop so that we never have
to. That's why we celebrate and rejoice: because we know Jesus
stepped in the gap, shouldered it all, and then turns to us with a
tender glance and calls us his child. We are his. We don't have to
hide anymore.

If you're reading this and you deal with cutting, please know
you are loved and God only wants to infuse you with grace, joy,
and beauty. You don't need to do that anymore. He heals. And
then you can point at the scars and say, "Look what Jesus did."

For me, sharing how Jesus has healed my past is a deeper level
of healing. Whenever I talk to others, there's a solidarity, a vulnerability, because God is there and healing takes place. Don't be

afraid to tell your story. Don't be afraid to show your scars. You may be able to bring light to a topic and help others who are still self-inflicting wounds.

Physical scars aren't the only type of hurting. The most painful scars we can't visibly see come from sexual trauma.

I get a lot of pretty personal e-mails, probably because Alyssa and I talk about relationships on YouTube, and one thing that comes up again and again is sexual assault and rape—and the guilt, shame, and grief that come along with it.

I don't think anything can hurt us more than sexuality being robbed, stolen, distorted, or misused against us. Sexuality is so intertwined with our spirituality and our very being, so those wounds are deeper than any other. If you speak with people who have suffered abuse in this area, they'll tell you how deep the feelings of shame and regret and hurt go. Even the apostle Paul makes the point that sexual issues are different from everything else.[4]

Recently I got an e-mail from a woman who had endured sexual trauma. When she was introduced to the idea of sex, she had made a commitment to wait for her husband. In seventh grade she even made a formal vow. As she got older and pressures ensued, she stayed committed and proud of the fact she was waiting for her husband.

The summer before she e-mailed me, she went out with some friends and later met up with a group of guys she knew. She only remembers having two drinks, and then everything goes black. Her friends headed to another bar but left her at the previous one. She woke up the next morning crying because she was so confused about what had happened the night before. Looking through her text messages, she saw that after asking her friends dozens of times to come get her, they did.

At this point she thought she might have been raped or abused in some way, but she said her friends assured her nothing had happened.

A month and a half later, she found out she was pregnant. She mentioned in the e-mail she was currently struggling to finish school and work enough to provide a good life for her baby.

Recounting her story makes me feel anger, sadness, and grief. Because in this broken world, sometimes wounds are caused by stuff we do, but (as in this scenario) sometimes wounds are caused by what others do to us. We did nothing wrong. Evil was done *against* us, yet we are the ones who have to deal with the repercussions. It affects us. It hurts us. It changes our lives.

And don't you dare be that person who says, "Well, if the victim had acted differently—." I've heard too many Christians take that line of reasoning, and I don't think anything angers me more. Plain and simple: if someone is raped or abused, it's not their fault. It doesn't even matter where they went, what they drank, or how they dressed. The evil was done by the perpetrator.

I came across a satirical article the other day that shows how ridiculous it is that we even have to say stuff like that. Caitlin Kelly, a web producer at the *New Yorker*, posted what theft victims' tweets would look like if they were treated as rape victims.[5] When someone's wallet is stolen and they say, "I think someone stole my wallet," our first questions aren't, "Do you have proof? Were you drinking that night? What were you wearing when this happened?"

If you're reading this and you've been assaulted, please understand: *It's not your fault.*

It doesn't matter what you wore, what you said, or how you acted. No one ever has the right to take advantage of another person's body. And to people reading this who maybe haven't experienced rape, let me say one thing: Please stop tying a woman's identity to her dad or brother or someone else. Many times when something happens to a woman, people will say, "What a shame. Don't people know that's so-and-so's daughter? That's someone's sister?"

We don't realize that we are subtly tying one human's value to another human's value to have weighted value. A person isn't valuable because she is someone's daughter or sister; she is valuable and has dignity and worth because she is an image-bearer. A human.

And this isn't a minimal issue. Because many guys watch porn and train their brains to think women are objects made to serve the man, their sexuality is so distorted that stuff like this happens in crazy numbers. Around 686,000 women are raped per year—that's about 1,800 *per day.* And on average one in five girls and one in seven guys are sexually assaulted by the time they are twenty-two.[6]

We are the first generation to have porn readily available to anyone at any time on a four-inch screen, so we are raising the most sexually exploited and sexually exploitive people in history. What's that going to do to us? Our kids? Our society? This issue is pervasive, and wounds continue to be made.

Whatever the wound is, something deep like assault or

something seemingly insignificant that still stings, know that healing comes from Jesus. He takes it, heals it, and gives new life.

RUNAWAY GOAT

There is an ancient Israelite and Jewish holiday called Yom Kippur, or the "Day of Atonement." Back when the temple still existed, the priest sacrificed one goat on an altar and sent a second goat into the wilderness.

The second goat has always fascinated me. According to the Torah, the high priest was commanded to put his hands on the head of the goat, confess Israel's sins, and transfer them to the goat. When that was done, he would send the goat out into the wilderness never to be seen again. This is where we get the term *scapegoat*.

But what's fascinating is Jesus wrapped up all these traditions in himself, and that scapegoat was only a shadow. The real thing is Jesus.

We are called to take the deepest, darkest, hardest sins of ours (ones we've done, and ones that have been done against us) and reach out our hands and put them on Jesus. On the cross Jesus was both the sacrifice and the scapegoat. He took our sins into the grave, as the goat took them to the wilderness.

The beautiful part is, once we transfer them to Jesus, he leaves them in the grave, resurrects, and shuts the door to death behind him. We have new life now. We have peace and forgiveness. We are new creations.

Have you had that moment? Have you leaned in and put that weight on Jesus? Are you tired yet? Tired of the shame, guilt, and game we have to play to keep it all together? He wants it, he takes it, and he defeats it.

And notice, too, that when Jesus comes out the other side, in the resurrection, his wounds are no longer wounds.

They are scars.

They've been healed. They tell a story. What's more, after the resurrection Jesus is in a perfect glorified body. (His body is what ours will look like at the end of time when everything is fully restored.)

Yet he still has scars. While many of us see scars as a weakness, if Jesus has scars *after* the resurrection, then maybe they're not. Maybe scars make us truly human. They show we've lived. They tell our story. Without our scars we might not be the same people, but praise God they are no longer wounds.

This is illustrated perfectly after Jesus rises from the dead and interacts with Thomas, also known as the doubting disciple. His friends were telling Thomas that Jesus had risen, but Thomas didn't believe them. "Unless I see in his hands the mark of the nails, and place my finger into the mark of the nails, and place my hand into his side, I will never believe."[7]

Eight days later, Jesus and Thomas finally see each other. Jesus doesn't rebuke Thomas and tell him to believe harder. He doesn't tell him to read more apologetics books. He doesn't say, "Just have faith." He says, "Put your finger here, and see my hands; and put out your hand, and place it in my side. Do not disbelieve, but believe."[8]

The answer to Thomas's doubt was Jesus telling Thomas to reach out and touch him. To feel his scars. It's almost as if

Jesus' scars were what proved his humanity. Made him real in that moment.

Many times we miss Jesus because we try to muster intellectual rigor or arguments in our darkest times, but Jesus simply says, *"Touch me."* There's intimacy there. There's Jesus saying in our pain, *"I know. Look at my scars."* He had experienced death, but he had also experienced resurrection.

Going back to the story of the young woman I previously mentioned, she summed up her healing perfectly when she said, "I've clung to knowing that Jesus has a plan for me. Every time I feel my baby move, I know that he has great things in store for me and for my son. He is my rock, and if I lean on him and the people he has put in my life, I can make it through anything."

Every time the baby kicks, it's God's way of saying, *"I'm bigger than evil. I'm bigger than what's been done against you. This is what resurrection looks like."*

Evil didn't win. There's new life bursting forth right in the middle of death, evil, and hurt.

CHAPTER NINE

THE TABLE'S NOT WHAT YOU THINK

IT'S NOT JUST A MEAL; IT'S A SACRED SPACE

YEARS AGO A MESSIANIC JEW, ILAN ZAMIR, WAS DRIVING through an Arab village in Israel, when a dark blur darted in front of the car. He slammed on his breaks, but it was too late. He struck and killed a thirteen-year-old Palestinian. Because he was deaf, the boy never heard the car coming.

Ilan was a follower of Jesus and immediately felt the need to seek reconciliation, make amends, and do anything in his power to seek forgiveness. Unfortunately, the relationships between Jewish and Palestinian people might be the most deep-seated, tension-filled ethnic divide in our world today. There are numerous cases of both sides committing grievous acts against the other simply because they believe the other is their enemy.

Haunted by the death of the little boy and his part in it, Ilan, however, was determined to make amends in any way possible. When he mentioned the idea to his Jewish friends, Ilan was met with disbelief. Even an Israeli policeman said, "That's dangerous what you want to do. You can get into serious trouble. You're an Israeli Jew, and these people you want to meet are Arabs on the West Bank."

Ilan knew how dangerous attempting reconciliation could be. After all, according to some Arab traditions, a family could kill him as vengeance. But after chatting with an Arab pastor, Ilan decided to arrange a *sulha*—a conventional meal used in Arab cultures to mark reconciliation. It's the equivalent of the Hebrew word *shulhan*, which means "table." So he set up the meal. Would they accept his apology and grant forgiveness? Would they yell at him? Worse, would they hurt him? But love takes risks, and so Ilan took a risk. As he describes it,

> The cups of coffee remained on the table, untouched. According to tradition, the father would be the first to taste from the cup as a sign that he accepted the reconciliation gesture, and had indeed agreed to forgive. The tension in his face had cast a shadow on the proceedings until then, but at that point he suddenly began to smile. The lines of grief softened. He looked at me squarely and his smile broadened as he moved towards me, opening his arms in a gesture of embrace. As we met and embraced, he kissed me ceremonially three times on the cheeks. Everyone began to shake hands with one another as the father sipped the coffee. The whole atmosphere was transformed, the tension at an end.[1]

Toward the end of the meal, someone at the table looked at Ilan and said, "Know, O my brother, that you are in place of this son who has died. You have a family and a home somewhere else, but know that here is your second home."

Can you imagine what a wave of love, grace, and reconciliation washed over not only Ilan but that whole table? There's a special presence and beauty in a moment like that no one can put into words.

What I love most about the story is how the word *sulha* means "table." In almost all cultures, except Western postmodern society, the table represents something deeply sacred.

It's a place of peace, of love, and of covenant. Whoever you sit with at a table aligns you with those people. Whoever is at the table together is, in one way or another, family. Some cultures take this principle so far that the leader of the home is responsible for protecting guests at the table at all expense—even if that means death. It is an honor, and hospitality was an art.

But sadly in our world today, we've lost that idea almost completely. Food is meant to be fast, efficient, and usually in front of a TV or with a phone in hand. Or it is fuel. Growing up in an athletic culture and playing baseball in college, food was changed from fast and convenient to scientific and biological fuel. It was calories and carbs and math.

We've lost the art of the table in America. One of the few exceptions is when families make it a point to have dinner together at least once a week, and refer to it as *family dinner*, a concept I find strange. Shouldn't it be a given that dinners are eaten together as a family? And shouldn't sitting down and sharing a meal be the most natural and basic part of our day?

For the most part in our culture, we no longer sit down to share meals, share stories, and share our hearts. We don't partake and use the beautiful sacredness of food as momentary temples or altars that they actually are. Which is exactly how traditional Jewish homes to this day see the table. It is considered a family altar, a little sanctuary where God can dwell.

What if we saw the table like that? What if whenever we sat down to eat at the table, which constantly reminds us of our need, we believed it was a little space where God dwelled? Where his presence is made known?

Yet the table meant family and peace in Jesus' day. That's why he was flatly condemned by the religious leaders for his dinner companions. They even smugly ask in Matthew 9, "Why does your teacher eat with tax collectors and sinners?"[2] Today religious folks might condemn Jesus followers for having tattoos or listening to secular music, but in Jesus' day they condemned him for eating with the wrong people.

Eating together meant intimacy. It meant friendship. It meant family. It meant peace, promise, and protection. J. R. R. Tolkien said that "if more of us valued food and cheer and song above hoarded gold, it would be a merrier world."[3]

There's something special about the table. Even how a table is designed is deeply symbolic. Everyone is sitting down. In some cultures everyone sits on the floor while they eat, and in others we sit at a table, but in both ways, everyone is on the same level. Everyone is equal. When you sit around the table, you are looking into other people's eyes.

Jesus knew the power of the table and used it in some unique ways. He never just provided spiritual facts, but entered into people's lives and let truth rest at the table.

NOT A THEORY, BUT A MEAL

Jesus dying on the cross, even if you aren't a follower of Jesus, can arguably be called the most impactful event in all history. It has changed more people, affected more people, and passed through cultures and languages more than anything else. You'd think Jesus would give quite possibly his best sermon or teaching to make sure the disciples understood what was about to happen.

He had been with them for three years and was now a mere twenty-four hours away from what it all was leading to. We would expect him to give every last drop of truth, spiritual points, and facts to the disciples to make sure they didn't miss what was about to happen.

When we read the account of the last night Jesus had with his disciples—men he had known well for three years—we expect to find the best sermon of his life, right? Or at least a huge all-night recap of everything he'd taught them the past three years. But there's no whiteboard, pulpit, or systematic theology book.

Jesus didn't say, "All right, disciples. Here's an outline describing atonement. You need to memorize this and make sure you understand the theological truth that's about to unfold."

He didn't do any of that. Instead, for the very last act of his life with his disciples, Jesus *ate* with them.

To describe the biggest event in human history, Jesus didn't give them a theory, a formula, or an equation; he gave them a *meal*.

He used bread and wine to describe the cross.

The table is a sacred space.

More than ever we need to learn the art of sitting at a table with other image-bearers of God. In a culture that is constantly dehumanizing or reducing people to profile photos, job titles, and failures, the table is a chance to restore glory. I see this firsthand with every person I interact with online.

Because I'm a public figure (whatever that means), I've noticed people can say things about me on Twitter, Facebook, and other places that I'm sure they wouldn't say if they were with me in person. And not because they'd be scared to (I'm not a big guy, so I'm not scary), but because it doesn't feel right to be rude to someone in person.

When we dehumanize, we are able to dismiss, belittle, and be rude. But face-to-face, even if we disagree with someone, it's so much harder to be dismissive or rude or caricature them because there's something in us that doesn't like to make others feel badly about themselves.

Talking about the effect of smartphones on children's social development, comedian Louis C. K. said,

> I think these things are toxic, especially for kids. . . . They don't look at people when they talk to them, and they don't build empathy. You know, kids are mean, and it's 'cause they're trying it out. They look at a kid and they go, "You're fat," and then they see the kid's face scrunch up and they go, "Oh. That doesn't feel good to make a person do that." But they got to start with doing the mean thing. But when they write "you're fat," then they just go, "Mmm, that was fun. I like that."[4]

The Internet is changing how we interact with each other, because with the Internet you can't see what your words do to someone else. You can't see the hurt in his face, hear the ache in her voice. When you do, it does something to you. It lets you empathize. Take a different posture. And lean in.

Where we are in the Western world, we need the table more than ever. It certainly isn't unique, though, and the reconciliation the table represents is needed everywhere. Everyone opposes someone else. Conservatives don't like liberals. Gays don't like Christians. Israelis don't like Palestinians. White cops don't like black teens.

Now of course these stereotypes aren't true across the board, but we've bought this lie and heard this narrative over and over again through media.

As I write there is a national uproar over the events that transpired in the deaths of Michael Brown in Ferguson, Missouri, and Eric Garner in New York. Millions of people are currently protesting.

The worst part is when people completely belittle or make zero effort to understand the angst and hurt and pain coming from my black brothers and sisters right now. We need to understand that it's a nonnegotiable for us to absorb other people's pain—especially if we are followers of Jesus. Part of the job of being a Jesus follower is making other people's pain our pain. To feel it. To absorb it. To step in that gap as much as possible, because that's exactly what Jesus did for us.

When I see others make no effort to understand, and simply spew rhetoric and put more value in who they deem to be right, as if that's all that matters in life, I am even more convinced that the table can provide a beautiful place of healing and reconciliation.

In national cases such as these, I am glad that the hurt, pain, and angst that has been there the whole time bubbles up and now has to be dealt with. What would happen if a group of white folks invited their black neighbors over for dinner and simply asked them to tell their story? Or if urban communities invited a few police officers over for dinner and asked them to share how hard it is to be a cop? I know plenty of pastors and leaders across the nation who took the protests as an opportunity to listen. To sit down. To ask questions. To eat together.

I'm technically Native American, but I am self-aware enough to know that I look like a white person or at least enough to get the privilege that comes with that. If Alyssa and I have a son, do you know it's twenty-one times less likely that he'd be shot and killed by a policeman than his black friend? That means twenty-one black teens would have to be killed by the cops for there to be a statistical possibility that my white son would be.

That is the kind of stuff you hear at the table. Don't be afraid to sit down and ask your neighbors, ask your enemies. Ask them to tell you how they've been hurt, judged, or maligned because of the color of their skin. Instead of assuming, ask and then listen. You'll be surprised what it'll do for your soul and for theirs.

The table isn't just a place of a meal, but a symbol of family. Of oneness. Of we-are-in-this-together-ness.

Rabbi Pinchas asked his students how one recognizes the moment when night ends and day begins. "Is it the moment that it is light enough to tell a dog from a sheep?" one of the pupils asked. "No," the rabbi answered. "Is it the moment when we can tell a date palm from a fig tree?" the second asked. "No, that's not it, either," the rabbi replied. "So when does morning come, then?" the pupils asked. "It's the moment when we look into the face of any person and recognize them as our brother or sister," Rabbi Pinchas said. "Until we're able to do that, it's still night."[5]

It doesn't work to stand on a street corner and yell at people. Instead, truth is when we sit at the table, facing one another and breaking bread. God has made the table a holy place. We aren't left guessing what the kingdom of Jesus looks like, when we can read what it looked like on earth. And one of the main components was Jesus *ate* with people. He sat down with them.

There is something mysterious and beautiful about the table. The table is scandalous and subversive.

While Jesus did a lot of eating with folks and proclaiming that the kingdom of heaven is near, we'd do right to follow suit. What if we invited those we disagreed with—or whose perspectives we are completely removed from—over for dinner?

HOW JESUS DOES BIBLE STUDY

In Scripture the table is closely linked with truth. It's the place of learning. The place of experience. The place of teaching. The people who care about truth should care about the table, because in Scripture you can't have one without the other. Only in our postmodern thinking have we put so much weight on mental assent and facts that would've been completely foreign to many cultures before us.

One of my favorite—and probably one of the most under-rated—stories in all Scripture is after Jesus resurrects. He was just crucified by the Romans, and all hope that he was the one to restore Israel was crushed. I can only imagine the feeling of dis-appointment for some disciples who had followed Jesus for years, just to see him strung up on a piece of wood like a criminal. A cru-cified Messiah wasn't a Messiah to any person in the first century.

Then Sunday happens. The tomb opens, blood starts pump-ing in his veins, and the whole earth shakes. Human history takes a radical left turn at the resurrection of Jesus. God's answer to the world's problem is Jesus, and he won.

You'd think the first thing Jesus would do after such a cata-clysmic event would be of epic proportions, but it's almost anticlimactic.

The Gospel of Luke describes two guys who are walking on the road to Emmaus, recounting all that transpired over the last few days. They were probably trying to process what had just hap-pened. While they were talking, Jesus joined them, yet "their eyes were kept from recognizing him."

Jesus asks what they are talking about. They then almost sar-castically shoot back, "Are you the only visitor to Jerusalem who does not know the things that have happened there in these days?"

Where have you been, bro?

They even go on to admit they had high hopes for Jesus and "hoped that he was the one to redeem Israel." They believe that was crushed the minute Jesus died. Jesus' words then become very sharp to the two guys: "Foolish ones, and slow of heart to believe all that the prophets had spoken! Was it not necessary that the Christ should suffer these things and enter into his glory?"

Translation: Are you guys stupid? The Messiah was supposed to die the whole time! (Maybe he could've cut the guys some slack since up to that time almost no one in all history had read the Prophets expecting a crucified and strung up Messiah. This reminds us that there are ways to read the Bible and completely miss Jesus.)

Jesus then "interpreted to them in all the Scriptures the things concerning himself."[6]

In Jesus' day, the complete Bible was what Christians call the Old Testament or what modern Jews call the Hebrew Bible or *Tanakh*. So Jesus himself, God in flesh, explained the *entire* Old Testament to them. Jesus literally began on page 1, and walked them through to the end, and showed how he was the answer the whole time, without them knowing who he was.

The very Creator of the universe was the one explaining the Scriptures to these guys. They weren't left guessing anymore. God himself was saying, "Look! This should've happened the whole time. Let's start on page 1 and I'll show you all the way through."

You'd think their minds would have been absolutely blown and they would have started seeing the matrix numbers running down the screen with scriptural truth, but nothing seems to happen.

They keep walking, and when they get close to Emmaus, they saw Jesus was going farther, so they asked him to stay with them for the night. In Middle Eastern culture it was an honor to have someone stay with you, especially if they had farther to go and it was getting late.

The first thing they did was sit at a table and have a meal. But something crazy happens: "When he was at the table with them, he took the bread and blessed and broke it and gave it to them. And their eyes were opened and they recognized him."

Jesus walks through the entire Bible with these two guys and nothing happens. Then he rips a piece of bread in half, and they immediately recognize him.

They even go on to say after that, "Did not our hearts burn within us while he talked to us on the road?"[7]

This almost makes our Western minds short circuit. The heart change, the opening of eyes, the revelation, the epiphany, whatever you want to call it—it didn't happen when they got all the facts; it happened when they sat at the table. It happened when they ate a meal. When there was relationship.

It's hard not to believe the table and a meal is important to Jesus and the Scriptures after hearing a story like that. But what's funny is that a lot of us would much rather have our eyes opened in the first scenario.

Our dream version of Christianity is having all the answers. Can't Jesus just show up in my room visibly and audibly tell me what to do and believe? News flash: he did to two guys, and it didn't help as much as we'd think.

Yet when they sat down with him, their lives changed.

Here's a hard question to ask ourselves: Would we rather have Jesus give us all the answers, or would we rather sit at the table with him?

Don't get me wrong. Truth is vital. The Scriptures are my favorite things to study, to listen to, to immerse myself in. But Jesus always, always, always couples truth with flesh. With intimacy. With real life.

Christianity isn't a college exam—we don't need to memorize and regurgitate facts. Jesus wants to open our eyes when we are sitting at the table building a relationship with him. One requires relationship, one doesn't. A sit-down meal is long, it's conversational, it's back and forth, and it's beautiful.

What if that was how we saw Christianity? No wonder Jesus himself uses language such as "wedding reception," "party," and "feast" to describe the kingdom of heaven.

Our dream version of following Jesus is to have all the facts. Jesus' dream of us following him is to sit with us.

Every morning when I open the Scriptures, part of me wants to just do it to check it off my list. I do it to get the answers for the day. But the days that are filled with hope, peace, and love are when I see that time in the morning as simply sitting with Jesus. Knowing him. Talking to him. Learning from him.

It's more of a discipline than anything. It requires so much effort for me to just sit there. To be silent and listen for a little bit, then talk to him and thank him for all he's done, and then to ask questions and ask for help. Prayer and Bible reading is a dialogue not a monologue.

The problem is, we don't see how pervasive the problem is in our Western Christianity. In almost every aspect of our Christian lives, we are trained to take the life, flesh, and intimacy out of everything and leave just a skeleton of facts.

Take Communion, for example. Most of us who have taken it, or seen it before, might differ on the specifics of how it should be done, but many of us still make it more abstract than it was originally created.

A mentor of mine really shifted my thought on this. He gave me an example I haven't been able to forget. Let's say you got transported two thousand years into the future (maybe we used the DeLorean again). Try to imagine what it'd be like the minute you start walking around.

Things would be so foreign and advanced and different, it'd probably be difficult even to survive. The first thing you'd do is look for familiar signs—in the same way we look for the nearest McDonald's or Apple Store when traveling (maybe that last one is just me). On your way you overhear someone advertise a huge Thanksgiving feast that night.

You immediately light up. Not only is it something familiar but you *love* Thanksgiving dinner. I know I do. The turkey (dark meat only, of course), the stuffing, the mashed potatoes, the pumpkin pie. But not just the food—the games, the time with family, the whole day hanging out, talking, watching football, relaxing, and dealing with that one crazy uncle every family has. (If my uncles are reading this, our family is the only exception.)

It's a beautiful, amazing time. There's so much to love about Thanksgiving, so when you hear there is a feast that night, you get all the details and get ready to go.

Later that night you show up at the address and go in. But it seems weird at first. You wonder if you're in the right place. It's a large room with one thousand people and a big stage up front. Everyone is facing forward, and you can only see the back of everyone else's head. To your left they are passing a little gold bowl down the aisle. When it gets to you, you see it has little tiny bite-size pieces of turkey in it. And to fit in, you take a piece like everyone else. Then comes the little tiny cups of sparkling cider, and you take that too.

Then a guy you don't personally know gets on the stage and leads people through taking Thanksgiving dinner. The guy to the left of you nudges his neighbor and says, "That Thanksgiving dinner was great! Best one I've had in a while! It really spoke to me."

You don't know if you should scream or face-palm. This isn't Thanksgiving dinner at all!

Well, *technically* it is if you believe Thanksgiving dinner is just the piece of meat and the drink. But if you know—as we all do—that it's the atmosphere, the people, the table, the time, the football, and the love, then you know that wasn't it at all. You'd think it's incredibly weird. They have all the ingredients of Thanksgiving dinner, but they've ripped the life and joy right out of the center.

And that's basically what Western Christians have done with Communion. I'm sure Paul and Peter would feel just as out of place taking Communion today as you would feel two thousand years in the future with the Thanksgiving dinner example.

The Last Supper was an actual feast. Jesus linked his death to a meal so that we'd never forget our need for it, since we have to eat all the time. He said, "Every time you break bread and drink wine, remember me."

And after the resurrection the early church restructured the tone of the meal to be celebratory in nature. It was a love feast.

Communion in the early church was a table. It was a place where everyone was welcome. (The only time it's mentioned in Paul's letters, he condemns the Corinthians sharply, for making it a country club where not everyone was welcome.)

It represented mutual love, sacrifice, and service. There they showed they were all equally in need of grace and forgiveness and would take the bread and wine together as signs pointing to Jesus and his death. It was a marker of Jesus followers.

We've come up with a version of Communion that looks more like the industrial revolution than it does the early church.

A TABLE THAT HEALS

As someone who's dealt with serious seasons of loneliness, brokenness, and even depression, one place of incredible grace is Psalm 78: "They spoke against God, saying, / 'Can God spread a table in the wilderness?'"[8]

Can God really prepare a table in the wilderness? To ancient Israel the wilderness represented death, ache, pain, and hurt. Nothing grew out there in the desert landscape. Like the Israelites in Psalm 78, I've found myself grumbling sarcastically or bitterly saying the very same thing. They weren't asking earnestly but to show they thought God *couldn't* do it. But when we ask God a question, sometimes his answer can surprise us.

One of the weirdest verses in the Old Testament is in the book of Hosea. Israel is rebelling and not worshiping God. And to remedy that he says, "I will allure her, / and bring her into the wilderness, / and speak tenderly to her."[9]

There's this strange romance there. Where Israel saw dryness, a place no one wanted to go, and a place that only represented decay, God saw something different. *Allure* is such a tender word; it's as if God knows there are some things we can only learn in the wilderness.

It reminds me of the stars. If you think about it, the stars are always out. In the daytime, if you look up, they are there. You just can't see them. It's only when it's dark that they shine, shimmer, and glow.

What if that's God? What if in the dark seasons, we looked up and saw his beauty? What if he glows brighter when we think everything is spinning out of control? Because if we are honest, we know that sometimes the best place to see the stars in all their glory is the wilderness.

And right in the middle of Israel's (and our) bitter or sarcastic questioning, God's answer is yes. He really does prepare a table in the wilderness. He prepares a table in the silence. He prepares a table in the depression. He prepares a table in the growing pains.

The God of the cosmos prepares a table for you and me. He meets with us and doesn't leave us out in the cold. He prepares a table right in the middle of racial tension in Ferguson, he prepares a table for Israelis and Palestinians, and he prepares a table for you and me. We are invited to sit, to eat, to learn, to laugh, and, most importantly, to love.

What a beautiful picture that God not only prepares a table for us, but he sits with us. He looks at us. God became man and dwelt among us. The Word bowed and pitched a tent in our midst.

You don't have to go searching for God because he's right there smack dab in the middle of any table where everyone is invited.

We are all in the family. We are diverse, we are unique, and we are all the very body of our King, Jesus. We share the same last name, and that's what matters. The saying goes that "blood is thicker than water," and that saying is true. But it isn't our blood that unites us but his. And what's best is, like a true family should, we are all invited to the table. The question is, will you have a seat?

The last time I was in Israel we were invited to a worship night. What I didn't know, though, was that it was an unadvertised secret worship night with some of the most influential Palestinian and Jewish Christians in the area. It had to be during a certain part of the year because that was the easiest for everyone to get through the border crossing and past the checkpoints.

At the top of their lungs grown men in both Arabic and Hebrew were shouting the praises of Jesus. I would have taken pictures or video, but it was strictly forbidden. Many people could've lost their jobs or even lives if others knew they were there with their supposed enemies. But it didn't matter I couldn't take pictures—I'll never forget it.

Hearing Yeshua (Jesus in Hebrew) and Isa (Jesus in Arabic) proclaimed in a room where most people had siblings or parents lost in the wars and intifadas was nothing short of amazing grace. Toward the end of the night, they began dancing. I got taken up front with some of the adult men, and we formed a circle with our arms over one another's shoulders and began dancing and singing.

I didn't understand one word they were saying except *Yeshua*, but I do know they were excited and couldn't contain their love for brothers or for Jesus. I remember looking to my left and to my right and seeing a highly influential Palestinian man and then a highly influential Israeli man, both singing and dancing and locked arm in arm.

I believe this is what heaven will look like. It's no wonder in Revelation the end of time is described as a "marriage supper of the Lamb."[10]

In one of John's visions he sees *all* tribes, and *all* people, and *all* languages standing before the throne crying out with a loud voice, "Salvation belongs to our God who sits on the throne, and to the lamb!"[11]

That's our end goal. We already know the end of the story, but here's the question: Is the trajectory of our life putting us there? Or are we on a different path?

The reason table and intimacy and story and temple and Sabbath are so important is that they are relational. You can't tell a story unless you have a relationship with your listeners. You can't have intimacy without another person. You can't enjoy the power of the table unless other people are there.

And what would our lives look like if we returned to that? So many young people are "leaving the faith" after they get older because they never really knew the faith in the first place. Or a better way to say it is maybe they never really knew Jesus.

It's easy to leave facts. It's easy to change your mind. It's easy to throw something off and forget it.

But it's awfully hard to forget a person. To forget a relationship. To miss not being known and loved and forgiven at the same time. That's what Jesus is offering and that's what we are invited to.

To sit at the table with him.

He invited us long ago. It's about time we take a seat.

CONCLUSION

A FINAL WORD TO MY FRIENDS

IF YOU MADE IT THIS FAR, LET ME GENUINELY SAY THANK YOU.
Writing a book is a battle of words, time, energy, and discipline.
This book specifically weighed on me because I have come a lot
closer to Jesus in the past couple of years through these thoughts
and ideas, and I desperately wanted to write in a way that would
do the same for you. By the time you reach that last page, I had
prayed you'd be closer to him, love him more, and see that this
thing called Christianity is a dance of mystery, truth, grace, and
beauty.

I have heard that the gospel is similar to a homeless person
who found bread and was going around telling everyone else
where to find it too. If you're worn out, tired, broken, then know
that we all are. But God is healing, restoring, and remaking us
and this world.

My favorite part about writing a book is that in this day and
age, it becomes a conversation. Because of the Internet and social
media, you can tweet or engage with me while reading or after
reading. Weird to think about, but before twenty years ago, you
couldn't do that. Well, you could have written a letter, but that
took lots of time and energy.

If you just finished reading this book, I'd love to hear from you. Thoughts, feedback, questions, or even disagreements. The cool part about the Christian faith is that there are no fans, just family. My social media information is below. Come say hi.

Twitter: @jeffersonbethke
Facebook: fb.com/jeffersonbethkepage
Instagram: instagram.com/jeffersonbethke

ACKNOWLEDGMENTS

TO ALYSSA: THANKS FOR ALWAYS BEING MY BIGGEST ENCOUR-ager and supporter. Can't imagine going through life, or even writing a book, without you as my better half. Love you!

To Curtis, Matt, Sealy, and Mike: Thanks for believing in me! None of this would have been possible if you guys didn't think I was worth a shot. Thanks for taking a chance on me.

To the Nelson Team: I always feel weird about putting my name on the front of the book because being behind the curtain it's obvious to me just how much of a team effort writing, editing, marketing, and releasing a book truly is. Thanks for being the best team in publishing!

To Angela: Seriously can't imagine writing a book without your help. The polish the book has in its final form is all thanks to you, and I feel forever indebted to you for being able to take my feeble, broken, and very often ADHD words and make something coherent out of them.

To the Pryor Family: Thanks for loving Alyssa and me so

well. Your mentorship and friendship have shaped us immensely in the past year. Rereading the book I realized how pivotal you guys were to a lot of our growth and learning as a family. Thanks for teaching us what it means to truly follow Jesus.

NOTES

Chapter 1: Your Story's Not What You Think

1. Even though it's a little different, the people who grew up in great Jesus-following homes might feel this way, too, since they didn't have crazy overnight conversion experiences. But remember, you don't need to know your birthday to know you were born. [Curtis Hutson, Salvation Crystal Clear, vol. 2 (Murfreesboro, TN: Sword of the Lord, 1991), 199.]

2. Let me be clear: these bracelets and similar tools are very helpful and have their place, but they aren't one-size-fits-all outlines of the gospel. We should take every opportunity to tell the biggest story we can, not always the shortest and most formulaic.

3. Genesis 1:26–27.

4. First saw this distinction in Jonathan Martin's *Prototype*.

5. Genesis 1:27, emphasis added.

6. Dallas Willard, *The Divine Conspiracy* (New York: HarperCollins, 1998).

7. David Franzoni, *Amistad*, directed by Steven Spielberg (1997; Universal City: Dreamworks Video, 1999), DVD.

8. N. T. Wright, *Surprised by Scripture* (San Francisco: HarperOne, 2014), 138.

9. "Changing Paradigms," RSA Edge Lecture with Sir Ken Robinson, June 16, 2008, RSA House, London, https://www.thersa.org/discover/videos/event-videos/2008/06/changing-paradigms/.

10. John 3:3.

11. Wright, *Surprised by Scripture*, 135.

12. God can and does use every means to draw us to himself. He is bigger than our ways but surely can use our frail, feeble, and sometimes distorted attempts to share his gospel. But his ability and willingness to use our failures for his kingdom shouldn't keep us from pursuing the best option and telling the better story.

Chapter 2: The Temple's Not What You Think

1. Isaiah 66:1.

2. Exodus 3:7.

3. Exodus 29:45.

4. Revelation 21:3.

5. Exodus 25:8; Leviticus 26:12; Zechariah 2:10; 2 Corinthians 6:16; Revelation 21:3.

6. 1 Kings 6:1; Chronicles 22.

7. Jeremiah 52.

8. Psalm 137:1–3.

9. Luke 19:44.

10. 2 Kings 9:9–10.

11. Matthew 24.

12. N. T. Wright, *Matthew for Everyone*, Part 2 (London: Society for Promoting Christian Knowledge, 2002), 65–69.

13. Matthew 21:13.

Chapter 3: People Are Not Who You Think

1. Genesis 3:7–8.

2. Genesis 3:9–11.

3. Genesis 3:11.

4. Later when God gives the temple blueprints to King David, the entrance to the temple was on the east side, which means people had to go west to enter the temple and draw near to the presence of the living God. It's as if God is saying the temple is this little space of Eden, of restoration. It had garden residue.

5. Psalm 19:9–10.

6. Micah 6:8.
7. C. S. Lewis, *The Four Loves* (New York: Harcourt, 1960), 121.
8. Walter Brueggemann, *Sabbath as Resistance: Saying No to the Culture of Now* (Louisville: John Knox, 2014), 26.
9. Except one small exception of him saying one syllable "hi" to a hiker he passed once.

Chapter 4: You Aren't Who You Think

1. N. T. Wright, *Surprised by Hope* (San Francisco: HarperOne, 2008), 29.
2. Luke 3:22.
3. Jonathan Martin, *Prototype: What Happens When You Discover You're More Like Jesus Than You Think?* (Chicago: Tyndale, 2013), 18.
4. Matthew 4:3, 6.
5. Luke 15:15–16.
6. Matthew 3:17.

Chapter 5: The Sabbath's Not What You Think

1. John Ortberg, *Soul Keeping* (Grand Rapids: Zondervan, 2014), 126.
2. Thanks to Curtis Yates for posing this exact question to me in the process of writing this book.
3. Kate Murphy, "No Time to Think," *New York Times*, July 25, 2014, http://www.nytimes.com/2014/07/27/sunday-review/no-time-to-think.html?referrer&_r=0.
4. Louis C. K., interview by Conan O'Brien, *Conan*, TBS, September 20, 2013.
5. Sherry Turkle, "The Documented Life," *New York Times*, December 15, 2013, http://www.nytimes.com/2013/12/16/opinion/the-documented-life.html.
6. Abraham Joshua Heschel, *The Sabbath* (Farrar, Straus and Giroux, 2005).
7. Abraham Heschel, *God in Search of Man* (New York: FSG, 1976), 417.
8. Colossians 2:16.

Chapter 6: Worship's Not What You Think

1. C. S. Lewis, *The Great Divorce* (1945; repr., San Francisco: HarperOne, 2009), 39.
2. XXXChurch, "Stats," http://www.xxxchurch.com/extras/ pornographystatistics.html.
3. Psalm 115:8.
4. Psalm 115:4–5.
5. Revelation 5:13.

Chapter 7: The Kingdom's Not Where You Think

1. I've read this idea multiple places but especially remember Michael Hidalgo's book *Unlost* where he notes Caesar had many titles that Jesus claimed for himself.
2. Matthew 4:17.
3. Matthew 8:3.
4. John 13:4–5.
5. John 13:12–20.
6. N. T. Wright, *Simply Jesus: A New Vision of Who He Was, What He Did, and Why He Matters* (New York: HarperCollins, 2011), 218.
7. Ujala Sehgal and Robert Johnson, "15 Facts About Military Spending that Will Blow Your Mind," *Business Insider*, October 14, 2011, http://www.businessinsider.com/ military-spending-budget-defense-cuts-2011–10?op=1.
8. Luke 19:42.
9. Matthew 5:43–45.
10. Most empires allow some form of freedom, knowing if they don't there will be an uprising. In Rome the culture was very pluralistic. They'd even adopt other gods, but it was all under the banner of knowing who was truly in power and in control. The Jews were free to worship and were even an exception to certain Roman rules, but they also were a people occupied and didn't have many freedoms they would have if they were autonomous. The shadow of Caesar always lurked.

11. Let me make clear that not all Muslims long for brutal, violent dictatorships. I know many peaceful, loving, and gentle friends of other faiths. But I do weep they don't know Jesus as the king of their life and world. I'm simply drawing the closest distinction to the culture of America in the twenty-first century and the landscape of the first century.

12. Brian Zahnd, *Beauty Will Save the World* (Lake Mary, FL: Charisma House, 2012), 217.

13. Isaiah 2:4 NIV.

14. Colossians 3:16–17.

15. 1 Timothy 4:4–5.

16. 1 Thessalonians 5:18.

Chapter 8: Brokenness Is Not What You Think

1. Thanks to John Mark Comer and his book *Loveology* where I first heard the difference between scars and wounds.

2. Ann Voskamp, "When There are Wars and Planes Fall from the Sky: How to Face the Problem of Evil and the Greater Problem of Good," *A Holy Experience*, July 22, 2014, http://www.aholyexperience.com/2014/07/when-there-are-wars-planes-fall-from-the-sky-how-to-face-the-problem-of-evil-the-greater-problem-of-good/.

3. Zephaniah 3:17.

4. 1 Corinthians.

5. Nina Bahadur, "If People Talked About Stolen Wallets the Way People Talk About Rape," *Huffington Post*, November 20, 2014, http://www.huffingtonpost.com/2014/11/20/caitlin-kelly-if-rape-were-a-wallet_n_6191588.html.

6. Roni Caryn Rabin, "Nearly 1 in 5 Women in U.S. Survey Say They Have Been Sexually Assaulted." New York Times, December 14, 2011, http://www.nytimes.com/2011/12/15/health/nearly-1-in-5-women-in-us-survey-report-sexual-assault.html?_r=0.

7. John 20:25.

8. John 20:27.

Chapter 9: The Table's Not What You Think

1. Ann Spangler and Lois Tverberg, *Sitting at the Feet of Rabbi Jesus: How the Jewishness of Jesus Can Transform Your Faith* (Grand Rapids: Zondervan, 2009), 139–145.
2. Matthew 9:11.
3. J. R. R. Tolkien, *The Hobbit* (1937; London: HarperCollins, 2012), 333.
4. Louis C. K., interview by Conan O'Brien, *Conan*, TBS, September 20, 2013.
5. Tomáš Halík, *Night of the Confessor: Christian Faith in an Age of Uncertainty* (New York: Doubleday Religion, 2012), 176.
6. Luke 24:13–27.
7. Luke 24:30–32.
8. Psalm 78:19.
9. Hosea 2:14.
10. Revelation 19:9.
11. Revelation 7:9–11.

FURTHER READING

BELOW IS A LIST OF SOME OF MY FAVORITE BOOKS THAT HELPED shape, guide, or inspire the particular chapters. Some are written by Christians, some are not. Some are easy reads, and some are dense, long, textbook-like books that give me a headache about every two pages. Because of this I haven't read every page in every single book below because of the academic/reference form of some of them. Some also have parts I might not entirely agree with, or would say differently. Regardless, I hope you pick some of them up and are encouraged by the pages as much as I was. There's nothing like getting lost in a good book, and below are ones where I've done just that.

Chapter 1: Your Story's Not What You Think
- *The Mission of God*, Christopher J. H. Wright
- *Surprised by Scripture*, N. T. Wright
- *Imagine*, Jonah Lehrer
- *The Tipping Point*, Malcolm Gladwell

- *The Divine Conspiracy*, Dallas Willard
- *How God Became King*, N. T. Wright
- *The Drama of Scripture*, Craig G. Bartholomew and Michael W. Goheen

Chapter 2: The Temple's Not What You Think

- *The Lost World of Genesis One*, John H. Walton
- *Reading Backwards*, Richard B. Hays
- *Center Church*, Timothy Keller
- *Pentateuch as Narrative*, John H. Sailhamer
- *Sitting at the Feet of Rabbi Jesus*, Ann Spangler and Lois Tverberg

Chapter 3: People Are Not Who You Think (Intimacy)

- *Sabbath as Resistance*, Walter Brueggemann
- *The King Jesus Gospel*, Scot McKnight
- *Freefall to Fly*, Rebekah Lyons
- *All of Grace*, Charles Spurgeon
- *The Four Loves*, C. S. Lewis
- *Loveology*, John Mark Comer
- *The Meaning of Marriage*, Timothy Keller with Kathy Keller
- *People Over Profit*, Dale Partridge
- *Scary Close*, Donald Miller

Chapter 4: You Aren't Who You Think (Identity)

- *Prototype*, Jonathan Martin
- *Tempted and Tried*, Russell D. Moore

- *Beloved*, Henri Nouwen with Philip Roderick
- *The Truest Thing About You*, Dave Lomas with D. R. Jacobsen
- *The Prodigal God*, Timothy Keller
- *Jesus Through Middle Eastern Eyes*, Kenneth E. Bailey
- *Sit, Walk, Stand*, Watchman Nee

Chapter 5: The Sabbath's Not What You Think

- *Soul Keeping*, John Ortberg
- *Alone Together*, Sherry Turkle
- *The Impulse Society*, Paul Roberts
- *The Prophetic Imagination*, Walter Brueggamann
- *The Spiritual Man*, Watchman Nee
- *Abide in Christ*, Andrew Murray
- *Sabbath*, Dan Allender
- *The Sabbath*, Abraham Joshua Heschel

Chapter 6: Worship's Not What You Think (Idols)

- *Counterfeit Gods*, Timothy Keller
- *Surprised by Scripture*, N. T. Wright
- *Playing God*, Andy Crouch
- *Limitless Life*, Derwin Grey
- *Gods at War*, Kyle Idleman
- *The Great Divorce*, C. S. Lewis

Chapter 7: The Kingdom's Not Where You Think

- *Unlost*, Michael Hidalgo
- *Simply Jesus*, N. T. Wright

- *Reading the Gospels Wisely,* Jonathan T. Pennington
- *Poet and Peasant,* Kenneth Bailey
- *One Thousand Gifts,* Ann Voskamp
- *A Farewell to Mars,* Brian Zahnd
- *Spiritual Leadership,* J. Oswald Sanders
- *Anything,* Jennie Allen
- *7,* Jen Hatmaker

Chapter 8: Brokenness Is Not What You Think (Scars)

- *Prototype,* Jonathan Martin
- *Rid of My Disgrace,* Justin S. Holcomb and Lindsey A. Holcomb
- *The Release of the Spirit,* Watchman Nee
- *Heaven,* Randy Alcorn
- *Redeeming Love,* Francine Rivers

Chapter 9: The Table's Not What You Think

- *Bread and Wine,* Shauna Niequest
- *A Meal with Jesus,* Tim Chester
- *From Tablet to Table,* Leonard Sweet
- *Every Bitter Thing Is Sweet,* Sara Hagerty
- *Tables in the Wilderness,* Preston Yancey

ABOUT THE AUTHOR

HEY EVERYONE!

These "about the authors" are funny things because they are usually filled with generic statements from a third-person perspective. And it's weird they exist at the end of the book since I'd say you guys already found out a lot about me by reading the previous 200+ pages. Also it's hard because it's not a conversation over our dinner table where Alyssa and I love to get to know people the most.

Regardless, I thought I'd go first to take away the awkwardness. As you read, because I couldn't help but mention her dozens of times, I'm married to my amazing wife, Alyssa. We live in Maui where Alyssa lived after college, and where she was living when we were dating. We have a beautiful little one-year-old named Kinsley and a yellow lab puppy named Aslan (I'm a big Narnia fan). Most days we hang out together as a family at the beach or outside, work on YouTube videos or podcasts together, or watch a few episodes of our favorite show *Gilmore Girls* (not sure I want that fact in print forever, but oh well).

Well, that's me I guess (hopefully not all of it!). Would love to hear your story, as it pertains to this book or just in general. My contact info is below. Feel free to ask, critique, question, or just say hello. Appreciate you!

Twitter: www.twitter.com/jeffersonbethke
Instagram: www.instagram.com/jeffersonbethke
Snapchat: jeffersonbethke
Facebook: www.facebook.com/jeffersonbethkepage
Youtube: www.youtube.com/bball1989